The Magnolia Bakery COOKBOOK

Old-Fashioned Recipes from New York's Sweetest Bakery

JENNIFER APPEL AND ALLYSA TOREY

PHOTOGRAPHS BY RITA MAAS

Simon & Schuster

SIMON & SCHUSTER
Rockefeller Center
1230 Avenue of the Americas
New York, NY 10020

Designed by Bonni Leon-Berman

Manufactured in the United States of America

9 10 8

Library of Congress Cataloging-in-Publication Data

Appel, Jennifer.
The Magnolia Bakery cookbook : old-fashioned recipes from New
York's sweetest bakery / Jennifer Appel and Allysa Torey ;
photographs by Rita Maas.
p. cm.
1. Baking. 2. Desserts. 3. Magnolia Bakery. I. Torey, Allysa.
II. Title.
TX765.A58 1999
641.8'15—dc21 99-37070
CIP

ISBN 0-684-85910-6

ACKNOWLEDGMENTS

WE WOULD LIKE to thank Carla Glasser, for creating this opportunity; our wonderful editor, Sydny Miner, for her support and insightful comments (and her love of coconut cake!); and the terrific staff at Simon & Schuster who helped put this project together.

WE WOULD ALSO like to thank our families and friends, for their endless support; our bakers, past and present, for their creative input; as well as our enthusiastic testers. Allysa would particularly like to thank the Aranow family, for her childhood baking inspiration. But mostly we would like to acknowledge and thank our wonderful customers, whose sighs of delight make all the hard work and long hours worthwhile.

CONTENTS

INTRODUCTION 9

HELPFUL HINTS 13

Muffins, Buns, and Quick Breads 19

Corn Muffins • Oatmeal Muffins • Blueberry Muffins • Dried-Cherry Crumb Buns • Glazed Breakfast Buns • Sour Cream Breakfast Buns • Apple Pecan Quick Bread • Cranberry Orange Bread • Poppy Seed Bread • Chocolate Chip Peanut Banana Loaf

Cookies 31

Chocolate Chip Cookies • Chocolate-Covered Log Cookies • Chocolate Drop Cookies with Heath Bars, Vanilla Chips, and Pecans • Iced Molasses Cookies • Peanut Butter Cookies • Peanut Butter Cup Cookies • Oatmeal Raisin Almond Cookies • Almond Crescent Cookies • Orange Vanilla Chip Cookies • White Chocolate Coconut Macadamia Cookies

Squares and Bars 43

Lemon Bars • Strawberry Oat Bars • Raspberry Crumb Squares • Vanilla Pecan Brownies • Chocolate Brownies with Cream Cheese Icing • Fudge Brownies with White Chocolate, Toffee, and Pecans • Butterscotch Cream Cheese Swirl Brownies • Caramel Pecan Brownies • Peanut Butter Heath Bar Blondies • Peanut Butter Fudge Brownies • Magic Cookie Bars

Layer Cakes 57

Old-Fashioned White Cake • Traditional Vanilla Birthday Cake • Lemon Layer

Cake • Coconut Layer Cake • Hummingbird Cake • Maple Walnut Layer Cake with Fluffy Maple Frosting • Apple Walnut Cake with Caramel Cream Cheese Icing • Chocolate Buttermilk Layer Cake • Devil's Food Cake • German Chocolate Cake

Other Cakes 71

Lemon Vanilla Bundt Cake • Chocolate Amaretto Bundt Cake • Chocolate Sour Cream Cake with Chocolate Chips • Poppy Seed Coffee Cake • Dump Cake • Pear Pecan Cake • Aunt Daisy's Fresh Fruit Torte

Icings, Fillings, and Frostings 81

Traditional Vanilla Buttercream • Chocolate Buttercream • Lemon Buttercream • Seven-Minute Icing • Cream Cheese Icing • Chocolate Glaze • Basic Creamy Custard Filling • Butterscotch Filling • Lemon Curd Filling • Caramel

Cheesecakes 93

Crumb-Topped Cheesecake • Caramel Pecan Cheesecake • Heath Bar Almond Crunch Cheesecake • Chocolate Almond Cheesecake • Chocolate Swirl Cheesecake • White Chocolate Hazelnut Cheesecake • Mocha Rum Cheesecake • Raspberry Marzipan Cheesecake

Pies and a Cobbler 105

Apple Crumb Pie • Blueberry Crumb Pie • Lime Pie with Gingersnap Crust • Pecan Pie • Sweet Potato Pie • Cheese Pie • Chocolate Pudding Pie • Nectarine Cobbler

Icebox Desserts 115

Lemon Icebox Pie • Peanut Butter Icebox Pie • Chocolate Wafer Icebox Cake • Chocolate Pudding Trifle • Cream Cheese Chocolate Pudding Squares

Index 123

INTRODUCTION

In an age of microwave, quick-and-easy, freeze and defrost, the Magnolia Bakery takes us back to a time when we simply did everything the old-fashioned way: using the best and freshest ingredients, mixing them with lots of love, and taking the time to produce delicious homemade treats. Customers often request to lick the bowl as we prepare our desserts in our open-kitchen format. Some call and ask which muffins have just come out of the oven and are still warm.

As two women passionate for the culinary and homemaking arts, we opened the Magnolia Bakery in 1996. Allysa and I wanted to express our desires and creativity through a business that emphasizes a slow-paced, wholesome way of life reminiscent of 1950s America.

The Magnolia Bakery came into being over a brunch conversation during which we expressed for the umpteenth time our mutual frustration with our jobs and lifestyles. We finally decided that something would be done about it and opened up a wholesale baking business in early 1996. We soon received very positive feedback from our customers. When a retail space became available in our favorite neighborhood, the western part of New York City's Greenwich Village, we grabbed the opportunity. The West Village seemed ideal. It is low-key and family oriented, a place where we can do what we love where we love it. Over the course of two months and with the help of an adept construction crew, we transformed an empty shell into a warm, cozy kitchen that feels "just like Mom's." We scoured the flea markets and vintage stores to buy just the right furniture, decorations, and lighting fixtures to create an inviting atmosphere. Most people who walk in say they feel as if they have gone back in time to "Mom's" or "Grandma's" kitchen, with butter, fresh eggs, and other natural ingredients in abundance, just lying about and waiting to go into the mixers.

In the three years we have been in business, our popularity has grown tremendously. With only word of mouth for advertising, people from all over Manhattan, the outer boroughs, the suburbs, and even as far away as Iowa order our desserts. There is usually a long line out the door at night and on the weekends, as people buzz around our store like bees in a hive, scooping up the last of our sweet creations. Many people in the arts are drawn to the Village and the Magnolia Bakery. Actors, supermodels, musicians, and other celebrities often hang out at the bakery, making it one of the hottest spots on Bleecker Street. But famous or not, *all* our customers feel a welcome sense of being home at Magnolia.

While the business itself is fast paced and hectic at times, our original aim and values remain the same—natural, fresh ingredients, carefully crafted with goodness and love. In a world filled with stress, deadlines, and overwhelming demands, it is comforting to hear customers come in and sigh, "Gosh, you make me so happy!"

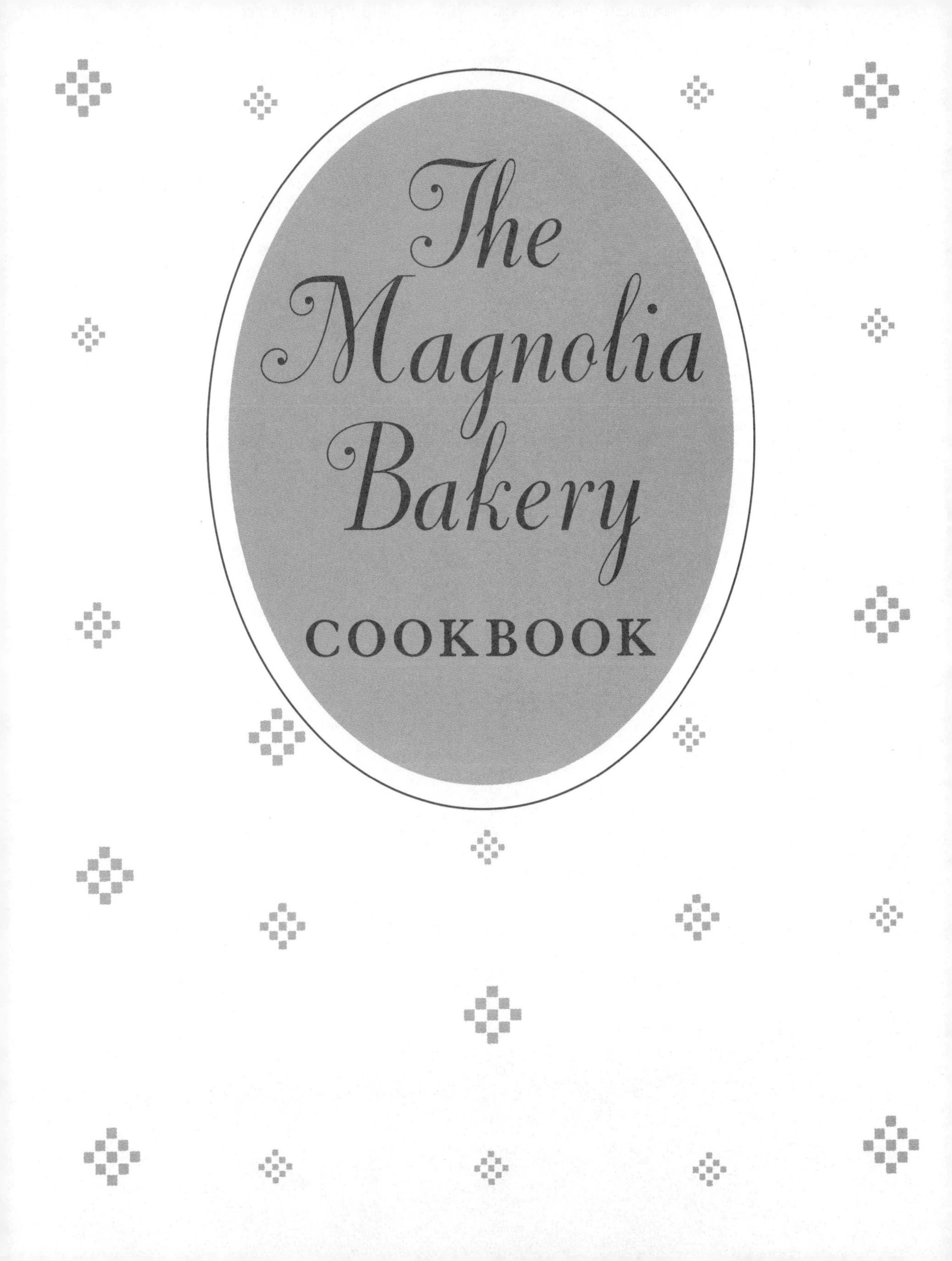
The Magnolia Bakery
COOKBOOK

HELPFUL HINTS

This section provides some suggestions to help you attain success as a home baker. While we have to produce large quantities of desserts at Magnolia, we still stick to the philosophy of home baking and follow certain rules to make sure our product is tasty and of high quality every time.

Layer Cakes

AT THE BAKERY, customers constantly ask us how we produce such tender, delicious layer cakes. Besides using the best and freshest ingredients, we adhere to a set procedure every time. By following our directions, you should be able to produce an equally luscious cake every time you bake.

We find it essential to be orderly. Follow proper procedure, measure accurately, mix carefully, use pans of the correct size, bake your cake at the proper temperature, and cool it properly. While this may seem self-evident, don't take these instructions for granted.

Before starting, always read through the recipe from beginning to end to ensure that you understand it thoroughly. Additionally, assemble all of the ingredients and the necessary equipment you will need before you begin baking, to make the process flow more smoothly.

Remove the butter and the eggs from the refrigerator at least an hour before starting the cake. The butter will be easier to cream, and the eggs will beat up better.

Select the pans in which your cake is to be baked. Metal pans should be smooth, because uneven or blackened pans tend to absorb heat unevenly. Grease the pans by using a pastry brush or by rubbing the butter or shortening with pieces of paper towel. After greasing, sprinkle a few spoonfuls of flour into the pan and shake it around until the entire inside of the pan is coated with flour. Empty out the excess flour by tapping the pan gently, then line the bottom of the pan with waxed paper or parchment. This is a foolproof way to prevent the cake from sticking to the pan.

It is best to bake the layers in the center rack of a preheated oven. Arrange the racks in the oven before preheating.

Sifting dry ingredients helps produce a fine-textured cake. If your recipe calls for sifted flour, it is best to sift the flour and then measure it. It is not essential for our recipes to do so, but it's a good practice to follow. After sifting the flour, add the other dry ingredients and sift all of them together.

When you are creaming the butter, it is paramount to beat until the butter is light and fluffy. Add the sugar gradually, beating all the while, and continue to beat for 2 or 3 minutes. Add the eggs one at a time, beating vigorously until the mixture is thick, fluffy, and pale in color. Up to this point it is almost impossible to beat the batter too much.

To make it easier to alternately add the ingredients, we suggest you thoroughly combine the dry ingredients in a bowl or large measuring cup and mix the milk, buttermilk, or other liquid together with the extract in a separate measuring cup. When adding the wet and dry ingredients, do so alternately, a small amount at a time, beating after each addition until the ingredients are blended thoroughly and the batter is smooth. However, do not overbeat or the cake will be tough. Use a rubber spatula to scrape down the batter into the bowl, making sure the ingredients are well blended.

If the eggs were separated, beat the egg whites until relatively stiff but not dry. Overbeating the egg whites can produce a dry cake. Pile the egg whites into the center of the batter and fold them gently into the batter, using a light up-and-over motion. Do not stir or beat, or you will lose the air in the whites, causing the cake to be heavy or flat.

Pour the batter into prepared pans, spreading evenly with a spatula so that the batter is level. You can use a measuring cup if necessary to ensure that you have an equal amount of batter in each of your pans.

Icings, Fillings, and Frostings

Before icing your cake, be sure the cake is completely cool. Icing will not stick to a warm cake, and a warm cake grows soggy if iced.

Brush all the crumbs off the sides of the cake layers and place the layers top side up (pan side down) on a level surface. Do not frost the bottom of the cake that was in contact with the pan.

Layer cakes should be frosted (or spread with filling) between the layers first. Then put the layers together, taking care that the edges are even and the cake is the same height all over. Frost the top and then the sides of the cake.

Frosting may be garnished in several ways: by additional frosting piped through a pastry tube or by using halved or crushed nuts, bits of candied fruit, shredded coconut, or sprinkles distributed over the surface.

Cookies

At Magnolia we like to make small cookies rather than the large ones seen at most bakeries and cafés these days. We find that they're exactly the right size for both children and adults, especially when you want just a small snack.

We like to play around with traditional cookie recipes and add our personal touches, such as the addition of a different chip, nut, or candy. Go ahead and experiment on your own, which adds to the fun and creativity of baking.

To achieve the soft and chewy texture of our cookies, we bake them at the minimum amount of time suggested in the recipe. For crispier cookies, we suggest you bake them for 1 or 2 minutes longer. Watch them carefully; you might burn the cookies.

Pies

Although it may seem a bit daunting to produce a beautiful golden flaky pie crust, with just a little bit of practice it is a relatively simple process.

Many of our customers approach us asking for tips on how to make a flaky pie crust at home or how to crimp the edges of the pie. We always tell them that it does take a bit of practice to get the feel of what the dough is supposed to be like. It also takes time to develop a light hand so that one works the dough without overworking it.

We use vegetable shortening in most of our pie crusts, because we find that it is easier to handle and that it produces a consistently flaky texture.

If you've never rolled out your own pie crust, it might be a good idea to start with one that calls for shortening instead of butter. Shortening is used at room temperature, and the dough is not chilled at any point, which tends to make it easier to work with. Butter crusts are a bit more complicated but worth getting used to because of their very flaky and moist texture.

Remember to handle your dough as little as possible, because overworking pie dough tends to toughen it. Start out with the dry ingredients in a bowl, then add in the shortening (or butter) cut into bits. Work quickly with a pastry blender to mix them together until they resemble coarse crumbs. When adding the water, make sure it is very cold (preferably ice water). Sprinkle the water lightly, but do not pour it in, because this will tend to produce an uneven dough, in that parts may be too dry and parts may be too wet. If the dough is too dry, sprinkle a little more water over it. With your hands, knead the dough together several times, just enough to form it into a ball. Flatten the dough and either roll it out right away for your pie or wrap it securely in plastic and refrigerate for up to 2 hours. We suggest using your dough as soon as possible to create the freshest, flakiest crust for your pie.

Cheesecakes

We love cheesecakes and continue to expand our variety as we experiment with different crusts, toppings, and ingredients. You too can mix and match your favorite ingredients, as long as you feel comfortable with the basic steps in creating this type of dessert. While cheesecakes are a delectable confection, they can at times be frustrating to create. We hope to help you avoid some of the pitfalls and offer some helpful hints to attain success.

An important step in mastering the technique of creating a rich and creamy cheesecake is making sure all your ingredients are at room temperature. This will help you mix your batter more easily and produce a smoother texture for your cake.

Most cheesecakes call for some type of cookie crust, mixed with melted butter and other ingredients. In order to create uniform crumbs out of cookies, we suggest you either grind them in a food processor or place them in a sealed plastic bag and crush them with a rolling pin.

Be sure to thoroughly and uniformly grease the sides of the cheesecake pan so the cake will not stick, as cheesecake tends to shrink when cooling.

An especially frustrating aspect of baking cheesecakes is the tendency for cracks to appear in the cake. If you have this problem, try some of these tips: Do not overwhip the cream cheese when beating, because this can cause too much air to be incorporated into the batter. Be sure to set the mixer on the low speed and to beat the cream cheese until very smooth before adding the other ingredients. Then, when adding the other ingredients, mix only until well incorporated.

Extremes in temperature can also lead to surface cracks. Avoid opening the oven door as much as possible while baking, and cool the cheesecake gradually in an oven that has been turned off.

Cracks can be avoided by using a water bath. Place a pan of hot water on a low rack in the oven below the cheesecake. The steam released from the water will provide moisture to the cake as it is baking. The water level should be checked about halfway through the baking time and the pan refilled if necessary.

Ingredients

Butter and cream cheese: Use the freshest and best brands possible.

Eggs: Always use large eggs.

Extracts: We suggest the use of pure rather than imitation-flavor extracts to obtain the richest flavor.

Flour: The recipes in this book were prepared with unbleached, all-purpose flour, except where indicated. Some recipes call for self-rising flour or cake flour. In these recipes be sure to use the flour that is indicated, because using a different flour will alter the texture of the dessert.

Lemon and lime juice: It is best to use fresh rather than refrigerated or frozen juice to obtain the best flavor. The same goes for fresh grated lemon, lime, or orange zest.

Milk: Our recipes call for the use of whole milk only.

Sugar: When we say sugar, we mean granulated sugar. When a recipe calls for brown sugar, it should be packed into the measuring cup so it will hold its shape when turned out (unless the recipe specifically calls for unpacked sugar). Powdered, or confectioners' sugar, if lumpy, should be sifted before being measured.

Muffins, Buns, and Quick Breads

Corn Muffins

In pursuit of the perfect corn muffin, we think we've got the right proportion of ingredients that create a light, moist, and not-too-sweet version of this traditional breakfast favorite. Maybe that's why customers call them the best corn muffins in town!

1¼ cups yellow cornmeal
1¼ cups all-purpose flour
⅓ cup sugar
1 tablespoon baking powder
1 teaspoon salt
2 large eggs, lightly beaten
1½ cups milk
¾ cup (1½ sticks) unsalted butter, melted and cooled slightly

MAKES 9 MUFFINS

Preheat oven to 350 degrees.

Grease well 9 cups of a 12-cup muffin tin.

In a large bowl, mix together the dry ingredients, making a well in the center. Stir in the liquid ingredients until just combined, being careful not to overmix. The batter may be lumpy.

Fill the muffin cups about three-quarters full. Bake for 18–20 minutes until lightly golden or a cake tester inserted into center of muffin comes out with moist crumbs attached. Do not overbake.

Here's an old-fashioned breakfast treat. The kids will never know they're eating their oatmeal!

2 cups rolled oats (not quick-cooking oats)
1½ cups milk
1½ cups all-purpose flour
1 tablespoon baking powder
½ teaspoon salt
¼ teaspoon cinnamon
2 large eggs, lightly beaten
½ cup firmly packed light brown sugar
½ cup (1 stick) unsalted butter, melted and cooled slightly
1 teaspoon vanilla extract

MAKES 12 MUFFINS

Preheat oven to 400 degrees.

Grease well a 12-cup muffin tin.

In a medium-size bowl, mix the oats and the milk and set aside for 10 minutes.

Meanwhile, in a large bowl, mix together the dry ingredients, making a well in the center. Stir in the liquid ingredients and the oatmeal mixture until just combined, being careful not to overmix. Batter may be lumpy.

Fill the muffin cups about three-quarters full. Bake for 16–18 minutes until lightly golden or a cake taster inserted into center of muffin comes out with moist crumbs attached. Do not overbake.

Blueberry Muffins

Nothing makes a cheerful morning like the smell of fresh muffins baking in the kitchen. These muffins originally called for whole milk, but substituting buttermilk really adds a special tangy moistness. Our friend Johnny Parker wouldn't think of getting on a plane to go away on business without at least half a dozen of these in his carry-on!

3 cups all-purpose flour
¾ cup plus 1 tablespoon (for sprinkling) sugar
1½ tablespoons baking powder
¾ teaspoon salt
2 large eggs, lightly beaten
1½ cups buttermilk
6 tablespoons (¾ stick) unsalted butter, melted and cooled slightly
1½ teaspoons vanilla extract
1½ cups blueberries, lightly coated with flour

Preheat oven to 350 degrees.

Grease well a 12-cup muffin tin.

In a large bowl, mix together the dry ingredients, making a well in the center. Stir in the liquid ingredients until just combined, being careful not to overmix. Batter may be lumpy. Gently fold the blueberries into the batter.

Fill the muffin cups about three-quarters full. Lightly sprinkle with the reserved tablespoon of sugar. Bake for 20–22 minutes until lightly golden or a cake taster inserted into center of muffin comes out with moist crumbs attached. Do not overbake.

MAKES 12 MUFFINS

Dried-Cherry Crumb Buns

Dried cherries give a new twist to the traditional breakfast crumb bun, and you don't need to worry about their being in season. At the bakery we have substituted fresh apples for the cherries at times, and even chocolate chips for a slightly sweeter version.

Buns
2 cups all-purpose flour
1 tablespoon baking powder
¼ teaspoon salt
⅛ teaspoon cinnamon
½ cup (1 stick) butter, softened
1 cup sugar
2 large eggs, at room temperature
1 teaspoon vanilla extract
1 cup buttermilk
1½ cups dried cherries

Topping
2¼ cups all-purpose flour
1½ cups unpacked light brown sugar
1 cup (2 sticks) unsalted butter, softened and cut into small pieces

Makes 16 buns

Preheat oven to 325 degrees.

Grease and flour 16 *large* muffin cups.

To make the buns: In a medium-size bowl, sift together the flour, the baking powder, the salt, and the cinnamon. Set aside.

In a large bowl, on the low speed of an electric mixer, cream the butter and the sugar until fluffy, about 3 minutes. Add the eggs one at a time, beating well after each addition. Beat in the vanilla extract. Add the dry ingredients alternately with the buttermilk, in three parts, beating well after each addition. Stir the dried cherries into the batter. Spoon the batter into the muffin cups.

To prepare the topping: In a medium-size bowl, mix the flour and the brown sugar. Using a pastry blender, cut in the butter until the mixture resembles coarse crumbs.

Sprinkle topping over buns, being sure to keep crumbs within muffin cups; otherwise they are difficult to remove.

Bake for 20–25 minutes until lightly golden or until a cake tester inserted into center of bun comes out clean.

Glazed Breakfast Buns

This delicate bun topped with a streusel glaze will definitely start your day off right.

Preheat oven to 350 degrees.

Grease and flour 18 *large* muffin cups.

To make the buns: In a medium-size bowl, combine the flour, the baking soda, and the salt. Set aside.

In a large bowl, on the low speed of an electric mixer, cream the butter with the sugar until fluffy, about 3 minutes. Add the eggs one at a time, beating well after each addition. Add the dry ingredients alternating with the milk and the vanilla extract, in three parts, beating until well incorporated. Spoon the batter into the muffin cups. Bake for 25–28 minutes or until a cake tester inserted into center of bun comes out clean. Remove from oven and allow buns to cool for about 30 minutes.

To make the glaze: In a small bowl, stir together the sugar and the water until smooth. Drizzle the glaze over the buns and sprinkle generously with chopped nuts.

Buns

3 cups all-purpose flour
½ teaspoon baking soda
½ teaspoon salt
1½ cups (3 sticks) unsalted butter, softened
2¼ cups sugar
6 large eggs, at room temperature
¾ cup milk
2 teaspoons vanilla extract

Glaze

1½ cups confectioners' sugar
3 tablespoons water

Garnish

1½ cups coarsely chopped pecans or walnuts (or nut of your choice)

MAKES 18 BUNS

Sour Cream Breakfast Buns

The comforting smell of brown sugar and cinnamon makes these buns a customer favorite. When our busy morning patrons grab one on the go, we like to think they'll have a peaceful moment in their hectic day as they enjoy it.

Bun

3 cups all-purpose flour
1½ teaspoons baking powder
1½ teaspoons baking soda
¾ cup (1½ sticks) unsalted butter, softened
1½ cups sugar
3 large eggs, at room temperature
1½ teaspoons vanilla extract
1½ cups sour cream

Topping

1⅓ cups firmly packed light brown sugar
2 cups coarsely chopped pecans
2 teaspoons cinnamon

Makes 18 buns

Preheat oven to 350 degrees.

Grease 18 *large* muffin cups.

To make the buns: In a medium-size bowl, sift together the flour, the baking powder, and the baking soda. Set aside.

In a large bowl, on the low speed of an electric mixer, cream the butter with the sugar until fluffy, about 3 minutes. Add the eggs one at a time, beating well after each addition. Beat in the vanilla extract. Add the dry ingredients and mix until just combined. Mix in the sour cream. Spoon the batter into the muffin cups.

To make the topping: In a small bowl, mix the brown sugar, the pecans, and the cinnamon. Sprinkle the topping evenly (and generously) over the buns.

Bake for 20–25 minutes or until a cake tester inserted into center of bun comes out clean.

Apple Pecan Quick Bread

Here's a terrific quick bread for any time of day. If there's any left over, this bread is great when lightly toasted and spread with some cream cheese. For an added tart flavor, substitute cranberries for half the apples.

1¾ cups all-purpose flour
¾ cup sugar
1 tablespoon baking powder
½ teaspoon salt
⅔ cup orange juice
⅓ cup (5⅓ tablespoons) unsalted butter, melted and cooled slightly
2 large eggs, lightly beaten
1½ cups coarsely chopped golden Delicious apples
½ cup coarsely chopped pecans

MAKES 1 LOAF

Preheat oven to 350 degrees.

Grease a 9 x 5 x 3-inch loaf pan.

In a large bowl, sift together the flour, the sugar, the baking powder, and the salt, making a well in the center. Set aside. Stir in the liquid ingredients until just combined, being careful not to overmix. Gently stir in the apples and the pecans. Pour the batter into prepared pan and bake for 50–60 minutes or until a cake tester inserted into center of loaf comes out with moist crumbs attached. Do not overbake.

Cranberry Orange Bread

Jennifer and good friend Peggy Williams bake this every year at Thanksgiving to bring to their family dinners. People always ask us for the recipe, and we've decided to share it with you.

2 cups all-purpose flour
1 cup plus 1 tablespoon (for sprinkling) sugar
1½ teaspoons baking powder
½ teaspoon baking soda
1 teaspoon salt
¾ cup plus 2 tablespoons orange juice
1 large egg, at room temperature
1 tablespoon grated orange zest
2 tablespoons unsalted butter, melted
1 cup whole cranberries, coarsely chopped

MAKES 1 LOAF

Preheat oven to 350 degrees.

Grease and flour a 9 x 5 x 3-inch loaf pan.

In a medium-size bowl, combine the flour, the sugar, the baking powder, the baking soda, and the salt. Set aside.

In a large bowl, mix the orange juice, the egg, the zest, and the butter. Add the dry ingredients and mix well. Add the cranberries and combine.

Pour the batter into prepared pan. Sprinkle the top with the reserved tablespoon of sugar. Add a few cranberries on top for decoration if desired. Bake for about 1 hour or until a cake tester inserted into center of loaf comes out clean. Let cool for 20 minutes before serving.

VARIATION: Add ½ cup poppy seeds instead of cranberries for a delicious orange-poppy bread.

Here's a great morning quick bread that can be enjoyed any time of day. We chose to make this in a tube pan so you'll be sure to have extra on hand.

2½ cups all-purpose flour
1½ teaspoons baking powder
¼ teaspoon salt
1¼ cups vegetable oil
1¼ cups sugar
3 large eggs, at room temperature
1 cup evaporated milk
⅓ cup milk
1 tablespoon vanilla extract
¼ cup poppy seeds

MAKES 1 BREAD

Preheat oven to 375 degrees.

Grease and flour a 10-inch tube pan.

In a large bowl, sift together the flour, the baking powder, and the salt. Set aside.

In a large bowl, mix the oil and the sugar. Add the eggs one at a time, beating after each addition. Add the evaporated milk, the milk, and the vanilla extract. Add the dry ingredients and mix well. Stir in the poppy seeds. Bake for 45 minutes or until a cake tester inserted into center of bread comes out with moist crumbs attached. Let cool for 20 minutes before serving.

Chocolate Chip Peanut Banana Loaf

It's the peanuts that add a bit of crunch and texture to this breakfast and teatime favorite. A healthy treat that's not overly sweet—enjoy!

⅓ cup (5⅓ tablespoons) unsalted butter, softened
½ cup sugar
2 large eggs, at room temperature
1½ cups mashed ripe bananas
⅓ cup milk
2 cups sifted *self-rising flour*
½ cup finely chopped, unsalted peanuts
¾ cup chocolate chips

MAKES 1 LOAF

Preheat oven to 350 degrees.

Grease and flour a 9 x 5 x 3-inch loaf pan.

In a large bowl, on the low speed of an electric mixer, cream the butter and the sugar until fluffy, about 2–3 minutes. Add the eggs one at a time. Add the mashed bananas and the milk. Mix in the sifted flour until well combined. Stir in the peanuts and the chocolate chips. Pour the batter into prepared pan and bake for 45–55 minutes or until a cake tester inserted into center of loaf comes out clean.

Let cool for 20 minutes before serving.

Cookies

Chocolate Chip Cookies

Allysa and childhood friend Beatrice spent many hours of fun in the kitchen and came up with this tasty recipe of their own in sixth grade. It sure beats doing homework!

At the bakery we sometimes add in 1 cup of chopped walnuts or pecans, or substitute vanilla chips or chopped Heath Bars for the chocolate chips.

1½ cups all-purpose flour
1½ teaspoons baking soda
½ teaspoon salt
⅔ cup (1⅓ sticks) unsalted butter, softened
½ cup sugar
½ cup firmly packed light brown sugar
1 large egg, at room temperature
1 teaspoon vanilla extract
½ cup miniature semisweet chocolate chips

Makes 2–3 dozen cookies

Preheat oven to 350 degrees.

In a large bowl, combine the flour, the baking soda, and the salt. Set aside.

In a large bowl, cream the butter with the sugars until smooth, about 3 minutes. Add the egg and the vanilla extract and mix well. Add the flour mixture and beat thoroughly. Stir in the chocolate chips. Drop by rounded teaspoonfuls onto ungreased cookie sheets, leaving several inches between for expansion. Bake for 10–12 minutes or until lightly golden brown.

Cool the cookies on the sheets for 1 minute, then remove to a rack to cool completely.

There's something so pretty and festive about these orange-scented chocolaty cookies. Roll them in a friend's favorite chopped nut for a tasty holiday gift.

1 cup (2 sticks) unsalted butter, softened
1 cup sugar
2 large eggs, at room temperature
1½ teaspoons grated orange zest
1 teaspoon vanilla extract
3¼ cups all-purpose flour
12 ounces semisweet chocolate, melted (see Note)
1 cup finely chopped nuts (such as pecans, walnuts, or nut of your choice)

MAKES 2½–3 DOZEN COOKIES

Preheat oven to 350 degrees.

In a large bowl, cream the butter until smooth, about 3 minutes. Gradually beat in the sugar and cream until fluffy. Beat in the eggs one at a time. Stir in the orange zest and the vanilla extract until well combined. Gradually add the flour until blended (dough will be crumbly).

Make a ball with the dough, flatten it, and then wrap in plastic and place in refrigerator for at least 1 hour (can be refrigerated overnight).

Remove the dough from refrigerator and let soften for 5–10 minutes. Taking small pieces of dough, roll them into balls and then 3-inch logs. Place logs onto ungreased cookie sheets, leaving several inches between for expansion. Bake for 10–12 minutes or until lightly golden. Cool the cookies on the sheets for 1 minute, then remove to a rack to cool completely. Meanwhile, melt the chocolate. When cookies have cooled for about 15 minutes, dip them halfway in the chocolate, then roll in the chopped nuts. Allow them to set for 15 minutes before serving.

NOTE: To melt chocolate, place in a double boiler over simmering water on low heat for approximately 5–10 minutes. Stir occasionally until completely smooth and no pieces of chocolate remain. Remove from heat and let cool for 5–10 minutes.

Chocolate Drop Cookies with Heath Bars, Vanilla Chips, and Pecans

Who says all chocolate chip cookies are created equal? These cookies have white chips in a deep chocolaty cookie, with toffee and pecans added to make them extra rich. Grab a glass of milk and enjoy!

2¼ cups all-purpose flour
⅔ cup unsweetened cocoa powder
1 teaspoon baking soda
1 teaspoon salt
1⅓ cups (2⅔ sticks) unsalted butter, softened
1 cup sugar
⅔ cup firmly packed light brown sugar
2 large eggs, at room temperature
3 tablespoons milk
1 tablespoon vanilla extract
1½ cups coarsely chopped pecans
4 coarsely chopped Heath Bars or chocolate-covered toffee bars (about 1 cup)
½ cup vanilla chips

MAKES ABOUT 3 DOZEN COOKIES

Preheat oven to 350 degrees.

In a large bowl, combine the flour, the cocoa powder, the baking soda, and the salt. Set aside.

In a large bowl, cream the butter and the sugars until smooth, about 3 minutes. Add the eggs and mix well. Add the milk and the vanilla extract. Add the flour mixture and beat thoroughly. Stir in the pecans, the Heath Bars, and the vanilla chips. Drop by rounded teaspoonfuls onto ungreased cookie sheets, leaving several inches between for expansion. Bake for 10–12 minutes.

Cool the cookies on the sheets for 1 minute, then remove to a rack to cool completely.

Iced Molasses Cookies

Gingerbread fans will adore this cookie. We sweetened them just a bit with some tasty sugar icing.

Cookie
2 cups all-purpose flour, sifted
2 teaspoons baking soda
½ teaspoon salt
1 tablespoon allspice
1 teaspoon cinnamon
¾ cup (1½ sticks) unsalted butter, softened
¾ cup sugar
1 large egg
¼ cup light, unsulphured molasses

Icing
4 tablespoons solid vegetable shortening
2 cups confectioners' sugar
2–3 tablespoons water

MAKES 3–4 DOZEN COOKIES

Preheat oven to 350 degrees.

In a large bowl, combine the already sifted flour with the other dry ingredients and sift again. Set aside.

In a large bowl, cream the butter and the sugar until smooth, about 3 minutes. Add the egg and mix well. Beat in the molasses. Add the dry ingredients and mix thoroughly. Drop by rounded teaspoonfuls onto ungreased cookie sheets, leaving several inches between for expansion. Bake for 10–12 minutes.

Cool the cookies on the sheets for 1 minute, then remove to a rack to cool completely.

To make the icing, combine the shortening, the sugar, and the water and beat until smooth. Cover until ready to use.

When cookies are completely cool, spread a thin layer of icing on each cookie with a small knife or spatula. Let icing set before stacking cookies, or they will stick together.

Peanut Butter Cookies

This recipe has evolved over many years of experimentation. We think, as do many of our customers, that we have discovered the secret to the perfect peanut butter cookie.

1¼ cups all-purpose flour
¾ teaspoon baking soda
½ teaspoon baking powder
¼ teaspoon salt
½ cup (1 stick) unsalted butter, softened
1 cup chunky-style peanut butter, at room temperature
¾ cup plus 1 tablespoon (for sprinkling) sugar
½ cup firmly packed light brown sugar
1 large egg, at room temperature
1 tablespoon milk
1 teaspoon vanilla extract
1 cup peanut butter chips

MAKES 2–3 DOZEN COOKIES

Preheat oven to 350 degrees.

In a large bowl, combine the flour, the baking soda, the baking powder, and the salt. Set aside.

In a large bowl, beat the butter and the peanut butter together until fluffy. Add the sugars and beat until smooth. Add the egg and mix well. Add the milk and the vanilla extract. Add the flour mixture and beat thoroughly. Stir in the peanut butter chips. Drop by rounded teaspoonfuls onto ungreased cookie sheets, leaving several inches between for expansion. Using a fork, lightly indent with a crisscross pattern, but do not overly flatten cookies. Lightly sprinkle cookies with sugar. Bake for 10–12 minutes. Do not overbake. Cookies may appear to be underdone, but they are not.

Cool the cookies on the sheets for 1 minute, then remove to a rack to cool completely.

Peanut Butter Cup Cookies

2¼ cups all-purpose flour
1 teaspoon baking soda
½ teaspoon salt
1 cup (2 sticks) unsalted butter, softened
½ cup sugar
½ cup firmly packed light brown sugar
1 large egg, at room temperature
1½ teaspoons vanilla extract
1½ cups coarsely chopped, chilled Peanut Butter Cups (9–10 pieces)
¾ cup peanut butter chips
½ cup finely chopped unsalted peanuts

MAKES ABOUT 3½ DOZEN COOKIES

Peanut Butter Cups, peanut butter chips, and peanuts—need we say more?

Preheat oven to 350 degrees.

In a large bowl, combine the flour, the baking soda, and the salt. Set aside.

In a large bowl, cream the butter and the sugars until smooth, about 3 minutes. Add the egg and mix well. Add the vanilla extract. Add the flour mixture and beat thoroughly. Stir in the Peanut Butter Cups, the peanut butter chips, and the peanuts. Drop by rounded teaspoonfuls onto ungreased cookie sheets, leaving several inches between for expansion. Bake for 10–12 minutes or until lightly browned.

Cool the cookies on the sheets for 1 minute, then remove to a rack to cool completely.

Oatmeal Raisin Almond Cookies

Here's another old-fashioned favorite with a nutty almond crunch. They're crunch-a-licious!

2¼ cups all-purpose flour
¾ teaspoon baking soda
½ teaspoon salt
1 cup (2 sticks) unsalted butter, softened
1½ cups firmly packed light brown sugar
2 large eggs, at room temperature
1 tablespoon vanilla extract
½ teaspoon almond extract
1¼ cups rolled oats
1½ cups raisins
½ cup finely chopped toasted almonds (see Note)

Makes about 3 dozen cookies

Preheat oven to 350 degrees.

In a large bowl, sift together the flour, the baking soda, and the salt. Set aside.

In a large bowl, cream the butter and the sugar until smooth, about 3 minutes. Add the eggs, the vanilla extract, and the almond extract and mix well. Add the oats and the flour mixture and beat thoroughly. Mix in the raisins and almonds. Chill the mixture for 30 minutes in the refrigerator before proceeding. Drop by rounded teaspoonfuls onto ungreased cookie sheets, leaving several inches between for expansion. Bake for 15–18 minutes or until lightly golden brown.

Cool the cookies on the sheets for 1 minute, then remove to a rack to cool completely.

Note: To toast almonds, place on a baking sheet in a 325-degree oven for approximately 10–15 minutes or until lightly browned and fragrant.

Almond Crescent Cookies

Jennifer sampled this simple and scrumptious cookie at a Christmas party. She was so delighted by it that the hostess gave her the recipe, which came from her grandmother.

1 cup (2 sticks) unsalted butter, softened
⅓ cup sugar
1 teaspoon vanilla extract
¼ teaspoon almond extract
1 cup finely ground almonds
2¼ cups all-purpose flour
Confectioners' sugar for sprinkling

Makes about 4½ dozen cookies

Preheat oven to 350 degrees.

In a large bowl, cream the butter and the sugar until fluffy, about 3 minutes. Add the vanilla extract, the almond extract, and the ground almonds and mix until all the ingredients are thoroughly incorporated. Slowly mix in the flour. Make a ball with the dough and roll small pieces of the dough into ovals, then form crescents. Place onto ungreased cookie sheets, leaving several inches between for expansion. Bake 12–15 minutes until lightly browned.

Cool the cookies on the sheet for 1 minute, then remove to a rack to cool completely. When cooled, sprinkle with confectioners' sugar.

Orange Vanilla Chip Cookies

These cookies were inspired by a recipe in Country Living *magazine. It's rather unique and reminds us of eating Creamsicles. People's mouths water over these! If you can't find vanilla chips, use white chocolate chips.*

2¼ cups all-purpose flour
¾ teaspoon baking soda
½ teaspoon salt
1 cup (2 sticks) unsalted butter, softened
½ cup sugar
½ cup firmly packed light brown sugar
1 large egg, at room temperature
1 tablespoon grated orange zest
1 cup vanilla chips

MAKES 2–3 DOZEN COOKIES

Preheat oven to 350 degrees.

In a large bowl, sift together the flour, the baking soda, and the salt. Set aside.

In a large bowl, cream the butter with the sugars until smooth, about 3 minutes. Add the egg and mix well. Add the flour mixture and beat thoroughly. Stir in the orange zest and the vanilla chips. Drop by rounded teaspoonfuls onto ungreased cookie sheets, leaving several inches between for expansion. Bake for 10–12 minutes or until lightly golden brown.

Cool the cookies on the sheets for 1 minute, then remove to a rack to cool completely.

White Chocolate Coconut Macadamia Cookies

All the exotic tastes of a tropical island wrapped up in one yummy cookie.

2½ cups all-purpose flour
1 teaspoon baking soda
½ teaspoon salt
1 cup (2 sticks) unsalted butter, softened
⅔ cup sugar
⅔ cup firmly packed light brown sugar
1 large egg, at room temperature
2 tablespoons milk
1½ teaspoons vanilla extract
6 ounces white chocolate, coarsely chopped
1 cup sweetened shredded coconut
1 cup coarsely chopped macadamia nuts

MAKES ABOUT 3 DOZEN COOKIES

Preheat oven to 350 degrees.

In a large bowl, combine the flour, the baking soda, and the salt. Set aside.

In a large bowl, cream the butter and the sugars until smooth, about 3 minutes. Add the egg, the milk, and the vanilla extract and mix well. Add the dry ingredients and beat thoroughly. Stir in the white chocolate, the coconut, and the nuts. Drop by rounded teaspoons onto ungreased cookie sheets, leaving several inches between for expansion. Bake for 10–12 minutes or until lightly golden.

Cool the cookies on the sheets for 1 minute, then remove to a rack to cool completely.

Squares and Bars

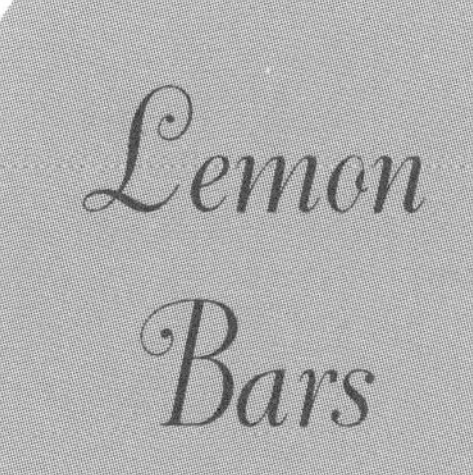

Lemon Bars

Jennifer formulated this recipe owing to the demand from our lemon-loving customers for a lemon bar. Hope our citrus fans approve!

Preheat oven to 350 degrees.

Grease a 12 x 18-inch jelly roll pan.

To make the crust: In a large bowl, on the low speed of an electric mixer, combine all the ingredients until mixture resembles coarse crumbs. Form the dough into a ball. Spread crust evenly into prepared pan. Use a large piece of waxed paper to firmly and evenly press down crust. Bake the crust for 18–20 minutes until lightly golden. Remove from oven and let cool for 15–20 minutes before proceeding.

While the crust is cooling, make the topping: In a medium-size bowl, on the low speed of an electric mixer, beat the sugar, the eggs, the lemon juice, and the zest until well combined. Pour over slightly warm crust. Return to oven. Bake 18–20 minutes until edges are golden brown. Remove from oven and let cool for about 20 minutes. Dust with confectioners' sugar.

Allow to cool to room temperature, or overnight, before cutting and serving.

Crust

2 cups (4 sticks) unsalted butter, softened
4 cups all-purpose flour
1 cup confectioners' sugar
½ teaspoon salt
2 teaspoons grated lemon zest

Topping

2 cups sugar
6 large eggs, at room temperature
1 cup lemon juice
6 teaspoons grated lemon zest

MAKES TWENTY-FOUR 3-INCH BARS

This versatile bar is equally delicious as a breakfast bar or a mid-afternoon pick-me-up. It goes great with a hot cup of apple cider.

Crust
2½ cups (5 sticks) unsalted butter, melted
4¼ cups all-purpose flour
1½ cups rolled oats (not quick-cooking oats)
¾ cup confectioners' sugar

Filling
1 twenty-one-ounce can strawberry pie filling

Topping
1¾ cups all-purpose flour
½ cup brown sugar
1¼ cups oats
1½ cups confectioners' sugar
½ teaspoon cinnamon
½ cup chopped toasted almonds (see Note)
1 cup (2 sticks) unsalted butter, softened, cut into small pieces

Makes twenty-four 3-inch bars

Preheat oven to 350 degrees.

To make the crust: In a large bowl, combine the butter, the flour, the oats, and the sugar, forming a doughlike consistency.

Spread crust evenly into an ungreased 12 x 18-inch jelly roll pan. Use a large piece of waxed paper to firmly and evenly press down crust. Bake the crust for 16–18 minutes. Remove from oven and let cool for 15–20 minutes.

While the crust is cooling, prepare the topping: In a large bowl, mix together the first six ingredients. Using a pastry blender, cut in the butter until the mixture resembles coarse crumbs.

When the crust is cool, gently and evenly spread the strawberry filling over the crust, leaving a ¼-inch edge all around. Sprinkle crumbs generously, allowing the filling to peek through. Bake for an additional 10–12 minutes until lightly golden.

Allow to cool to room temperature, or overnight, before cutting and serving.

Note: To toast almonds, place on a baking sheet in a 325-degree oven for approximately 10–15 minutes or until lightly browned and fragrant.

This scrumptious bar is a perfect blend of fruit and crumb. Serve it with a dollop of whipped cream if you like. You can try any of your favorite preserves as a filling; you can't go wrong!

Crust
2 cups (4 sticks) unsalted butter, melted
4 cups all-purpose flour

Filling
1¼ cups raspberry preserves (beaten smooth with a mixer or a spoon)

Topping
4½ cups all-purpose flour
3 cups unpacked light brown sugar
2 cups (4 sticks) unsalted butter, softened, cut into small pieces

MAKES TWENTY-FOUR 3-INCH SQUARES

Preheat oven to 350 degrees.

To make the crust: In a large bowl, combine the butter with the flour until you get a doughlike consistency.

Spread crust evenly into an ungreased 12 x 18-inch jelly roll pan. Use a large piece of waxed paper to firmly and evenly press down crust. Bake the crust for 15 minutes. Remove from oven and let cool completely, 30–40 minutes.

While the crust is cooling, prepare the topping: Mix the flour and the brown sugar. Using a pastry blender, cut in the butter until the mixture resembles coarse crumbs.

When the crust is cool, gently and evenly spread the raspberry preserves over the crust, leaving a ¼-inch edge all around. Sprinkle crumbs generously over the preserves (it will seem like more than you think you need).

Bake for an additional 15–18 minutes until golden brown.

Allow to cool to room temperature, or overnight, before cutting and serving.

Vanilla Pecan Brownies

This fabulous square is a double treat for vanilla lovers, with vanilla chips melted in and plenty sprinkled on top. The pecans lend a delightful crunch.

Brownie
1⅓ cups (2⅔ sticks) unsalted butter, melted
2 cups vanilla chips
6 large eggs
1⅓ cups sugar
1 tablespoon vanilla extract
2⅔ cups all-purpose flour
½ teaspoon salt

Topping
1 cup vanilla chips
¾ cup chopped pecans

Makes twenty-four 3-inch brownies

Preheat oven to 350 degrees.

Grease a 12 x 18-inch jelly roll pan.

In a medium-size saucepan, melt the butter with 2 cups of the vanilla chips over low heat, stirring often. Remove from heat and cool for 5–10 minutes.

In a large bowl, on the low speed of an electric mixer, beat the eggs until light and creamy, about 3 minutes. Gradually add the sugar. Beat in the vanilla chip mixture. Add the vanilla extract and beat until smooth.

Add the flour and the salt, beating until well combined. Pour the batter into prepared pan. Sprinkle additional 1 cup vanilla chips and ¾ cup pecans evenly over brownie batter.

Bake for 18–22 minutes or until a cake tester inserted into center of pan comes out with moist crumbs attached.

Allow to cool to room temperature, or overnight, before cutting and serving.

Chocolate Brownies with Cream Cheese Icing

This cakey brownie will delight chocolate lovers from coast to coast. If you ice half the pan with cream cheese icing and the other half with our variation fudge frosting, you might not know which one to choose. Better yet, ice one brownie with both icings and you can have your cake and eat it, too!

Brownie
3 cups cake flour (not *self-rising flour)*
1½ teaspoons baking powder
1½ teaspoons salt
1½ cups (3 sticks) unsalted butter, softened
3 cups sugar
6 large eggs, at room temperature
1 tablespoon vanilla extract
9 ounces unsweetened chocolate, melted (see Note)

Icing
1 pound (2 eight-ounce packages) cream cheese, softened
6 tablespoons (¾ stick) unsalted butter, softened
1½ teaspoons vanilla extract
6 cups confectioners' sugar

Garnish (optional)
¾ cup coarsely chopped walnuts

Makes twenty-four 3-inch brownies

Preheat oven to 350 degrees.

Grease a 12 x 18-inch jelly roll pan.

To make the brownie: In a large bowl, sift together the flour, the baking powder, and the salt. Set aside.

In a large bowl, cream the butter and the sugar until fluffy, about 3 minutes. Lightly beat the eggs, then add to the creamed mixture and mix well. Add the vanilla extract. Add the chocolate and mix until well incorporated. Add the dry ingredients. Pour the batter into prepared pan. Bake 25–30 minutes or until a cake tester inserted into center of pan comes out with moist crumbs attached.

To make the icing: In a medium-size bowl, on the medium speed of an electric mixer, beat together the cream cheese and the butter until smooth, about 3 minutes. Add the vanilla extract. Gradually add the sugar and beat until well incorporated.

Let brownies cool completely, then ice with cream cheese icing.

As an optional icing, try this fudge frosting: In a small saucepan, combine ¾ cup heavy cream and 12 ounces semisweet chocolate and place over very low heat. Stir constantly until smooth. Remove from heat and stir in ¾ cup confectioners' sugar until dissolved. Allow to stand until firm.

Note: To melt chocolate, place in a double boiler over simmering water on low heat for approximately 5–10 minutes. Stir occasionally until completely smooth and no pieces of chocolate remain. Remove from heat and let cool for 5–10 minutes.

Fudge Brownies with White Chocolate, Toffee, and Pecans

Quite possibly the richest and darkest chocolate brownie you'll ever taste. The mother of one of our employees will forgo her diet every time she visits Magnolia to have one of these. Don't worry, Mrs. W., we're sure you're not alone!

Brownie
1 cup all-purpose flour
1½ teaspoons baking powder
¾ teaspoon salt
12 ounces unsweetened chocolate
1 cup (2 sticks) unsalted butter
3 cups sugar
6 large eggs, at room temperature
2 tablespoons vanilla extract

Topping
¾ cup toffee pieces
¾ cup finely chopped pecans
1½ cups white chocolate, coarsely chopped

MAKES TWENTY-FOUR 3-INCH BROWNIES

Preheat oven to 350 degrees.

Grease a 12 x 18-inch jelly roll pan.

To make the brownie: In a large bowl, sift together the flour, the baking powder, and the salt. Set aside.

In a medium-size saucepan over low heat, melt the chocolate with the butter, stirring occasionally until smooth. Cool for 5–10 minutes. Transfer this mixture to a large bowl and mix in the sugar, the eggs, and the vanilla extract. Add the dry ingredients. Pour the batter into prepared pan. Sprinkle the toffee and the pecans evenly over the batter. Bake 25–28 minutes or until a cake tester inserted into center of pan comes out with moist crumbs attached. Do not overbake.

Let cool for 20 minutes, then sprinkle the white chocolate chunks over the brownies.

Allow to cool to room temperature, or overnight, before cutting and serving.

Butterscotch Cream Cheese Swirl Brownies

Here's a unique brownie for butterscotch fans. The cream cheese balances out the sweetness of the butterscotch nicely. Your mouth will be watering in no time!

Cream Cheese Filling
8 ounces (1 package) cream cheese, softened
¼ cup sugar
1 large egg, at room temperature
2 tablespoons all-purpose flour

Brownie
2 cups all-purpose flour
2 teaspoons baking powder
½ teaspoon salt
2 cups butterscotch chips
½ cup (1 stick) unsalted butter
2 cups firmly packed light brown sugar
4 large eggs, at room temperature
1 teaspoon vanilla extract
1 cup coarsely chopped walnuts

Preheat oven to 350 degrees.

Grease and flour a 12 x 18-inch jelly roll pan.

To prepare the cream cheese filling: In a medium-size bowl, beat the cream cheese and the sugar until smooth. Add the egg and beat well. Add the flour and beat until incorporated. Set aside.

To make the brownie: In a large bowl, sift together the flour, the baking powder, and the salt. Set aside.

In a medium-size saucepan over low heat, melt the butterscotch chips and the butter, stirring occasionally until smooth. Remove from heat and beat in the brown sugar until well blended. Allow to cool for 5 minutes.

Beat the eggs one at a time into the butterscotch mixture. Add the vanilla extract. Add the dry ingredients, beating until well combined. Stir in the walnuts. Pour the batter into prepared pan.

Drop the cream cheese mixture by teaspoonfuls over the batter. Using a small knife, swirl the cream cheese into the batter, forming a decorative pattern. Bake for 25–30 minutes or until a cake tester inserted into center of pan comes out with moist crumbs attached. Do not overbake.

Allow to cool to room temperature, or overnight, before cutting and serving.

Makes twenty-four 3-inch brownies

Caramel Pecan Brownies

These cakelike brownies combine with a graham cracker crust and crunchy caramel topping to taste almost like candy. You'll be tempted to lick your fingers. Go ahead—we won't tell!

Crust
4½ cups graham cracker crumbs
1½ cups (3 sticks) unsalted butter, melted

Brownie
2⅔ cups all-purpose flour
2 teaspoons baking powder
1 teaspoon salt
8 ounces unsweetened chocolate
1⅓ cups (2⅔ sticks) unsalted butter
8 large eggs, at room temperature
4 cups sugar
4 teaspoons vanilla extract

Topping
1½ cups coarsely chopped pecans
¾ cup cold Caramel (see recipe on p. 92)

Makes twenty-four 3-inch brownies

Preheat oven to 350 degrees.

To make the crust: In a medium-size bowl, combine the graham cracker crumbs with the melted butter. Press firmly into an ungreased 12 x 18-inch jelly roll pan.

To make the brownie: In a large bowl, sift together the flour, the baking powder, and the salt. Set aside.

In a medium-size saucepan over low heat, melt the chocolate and the butter, stirring occasionally until smooth. Remove from heat and cool for 5–10 minutes.

Meanwhile, beat the eggs until light and creamy, about 2–3 minutes. Gradually add the sugar. Add the chocolate mixture and mix well. Add the sifted dry ingredients, beating until well combined. Add the vanilla extract. Pour the batter into prepared crust. Sprinkle the pecans over the batter. Bake 30–35 minutes or until a cake tester inserted into center of pan comes out with moist crumbs attached. Do not overbake.

When completely cooled, drizzle Caramel over brownies.

While experimenting with recipes for this book, Allysa developed this variation on the traditional blondie. If you're a peanut butter lover, you'll be crazy about these!

Blondies
1½ cups (3 sticks) unsalted butter, softened
1½ cups smooth peanut butter
2½ cups sugar
3 large eggs, at room temperature
2 tablespoons vanilla extract
3 cups self-rising flour

Topping
1 cup peanut butter chips
3 tablespoons heavy cream
4 coarsely chopped Heath Bars or chocolate-covered toffee bars (about 1 cup)
½ cup finely chopped unsalted peanuts

MAKES TWENTY-FOUR 3-INCH BLONDIES

Preheat oven to 325 degrees.

Grease and flour a 12 x 18-inch jelly roll pan.

In a large bowl, beat together the butter and the peanut butter until fluffy. Add the sugar and beat until smooth. Add the eggs and the vanilla extract and mix well. Add the flour and beat until well incorporated. Spread the batter evenly into prepared pan. Bake for 25–30 minutes or until a cake tester inserted into center of pan comes out with moist crumbs attached. Cool to room temperature.

To prepare the topping: In a small saucepan over medium heat, melt the peanut butter chips and the cream, stirring until smooth. Drizzle the peanut butter mixture decoratively over the cooled blondies. Sprinkle the Heath Bars and the peanuts on top.

Allow to cool to room temperature, or overnight, before cutting and serving.

Peanut Butter Fudge Brownies

Remember the old peanut butter versus chocolate argument? You don't have to decide—you can have an abundance of both in this unbelievable brownie!

Crust
1¼ cups (2½ sticks) unsalted butter, melted
3⅓ cups all-purpose flour
⅔ cup confectioners' sugar
⅔ cup finely chopped peanuts
¼ teaspoon salt

Peanut Butter Filling
4 ounces (½ package) cream cheese, softened
⅔ cup smooth peanut butter
6 tablespoons sugar
1 egg
¼ cup milk

Brownie
1 cup all-purpose flour
1 teaspoon baking powder
½ teaspoon salt
½ cup (1 stick) unsalted butter, softened
2 cups sugar

Preheat oven to 350 degrees.

To make the crust: In a large bowl, combine all the ingredients. Form the dough into a ball and press firmly into an ungreased 12 x 18-inch jelly roll pan. Bake the crust for 10 minutes. Remove from oven and let cool for 15–20 minutes before proceeding.

Meanwhile, prepare the peanut butter filling: In a large bowl, on the low speed of an electric mixer, beat the cream cheese and the peanut butter until smooth. Beat in the sugar, the egg, and the milk until well incorporated. Set aside.

To make the brownie: In a medium-size bowl, sift together the flour, the baking powder, and the salt. Set aside.

In a large bowl, cream the butter and the sugar until fluffy, about 3 minutes. Add the eggs and the vanilla extract. Add the chocolate and mix until well incorporated. Add the dry ingredients. Stir in the peanut butter chips.

Reserve 1 cup of the brownie batter. Spread the rest of the brownie batter evenly over the cooled crust. Drop the peanut butter filling by large spoonfuls randomly over the entire surface of the brownie batter, being sure that some are close to the edges of the pan. Next, spoon out the reserved brownie batter close to some of the peanut butter filling. Using the tip of a sharp knife, swirl the two batters together to form a marble-like effect.

Bake 25–30 minutes or until a cake tester inserted into center of brownie comes out with moist crumbs attached. Remove from oven and immediately sprinkle the peanut butter chips evenly over top.

Allow to cool to room temperature, or overnight, before cutting and serving.

NOTE: To melt chocolate, place in a double boiler over simmering water on low heat for approximately 5–10 minutes. Stir occasionally until completely smooth and no pieces of chocolate remain. Remove from heat and let cool for 5–10 minutes.

4 large eggs, at room temperature
1 tablespoon plus 1 teaspoon vanilla extract
6 ounces unsweetened chocolate, melted (see Note)
½ cup peanut butter chips

Garnish

¾ cup peanut butter chips

MAKES TWENTY-FOUR 3-INCH BROWNIES

Magic Cookie Bars

In Texas these bars are called Hello Dollys. No matter what you call them, they're a huge childhood favorite whose popularity "will never go away again"!

4½ cups graham cracker crumbs
1½ cups (3 sticks) unsalted butter, melted
2 cups chopped walnuts
1 cups miniature chocolate chips
4½ cups sweetened, shredded coconut
3 fourteen-ounce cans sweetened condensed milk

MAKES TWENTY-FOUR 3-INCH BARS

Preheat oven to 325 degrees.

To make the crust: In a large bowl, combine the graham cracker crumbs with the melted butter. Press firmly into an ungreased 12 x 18-inch jelly roll pan.

Sprinkle over this the walnuts, then the chocolate chips, and then the coconut. On top, pour over three cans of sweetened condensed milk evenly, to completely cover the coconut. Use a spatula to spread if necessary.

Bake for 30–35 minutes or until lightly golden. Do not overbake.

Allow to cool to room temperature, or overnight, before cutting and serving.

Layer Cakes

Here's a terrific cake with a wonderful texture. It uses only egg whites, so it's ideal for the cholesterol-conscious. Try it with as many icings as you can think of—you can't go wrong!

½ cup (1 stick) unsalted butter, softened
1½ cups sugar
2 cups self-rising flour
1 cup milk
2 teaspoons vanilla extract
4 large egg whites

MAKES 1 TWO-LAYER 9-INCH CAKE

Preheat oven to 350 degrees.

Grease and lightly flour two 9 x 2-inch round cake pans, then line the bottoms with waxed paper.

To make the cake: In a large bowl, on the medium speed of an electric mixer, cream the butter until smooth. Add the sugar gradually and beat until fluffy, about 3 minutes. Add the flour in three parts, alternating with the milk and the vanilla extract, beating well after each addition. In a separate bowl, on the high speed of an electric mixer, beat the egg whites until soft peaks form. Gently fold into batter, making sure no streaks of whites are showing. Divide batter between the cake pans. Bake for 22–25 minutes or until a cake tester inserted into center of cake comes out clean. Let cakes cool in pans for 10 minutes. Remove from pans and cool completely on wire rack.

When cake has cooled, ice between the layers, then ice top and sides of cake.

Traditional Vanilla Birthday Cake

At Magnolia we decided to make our cake not quite a traditional yellow cake or a traditional sponge cake, given the use of whole eggs in our recipe. We're sure you'll agree this recipe is moist, delicious, and makes a beautiful layer cake or cupcakes for birthdays or any celebration. Frost with pink buttercream icing and lots of colored sprinkles as we do, and feel as though you're at your seventh birthday party all over again!

1 cup (2 sticks) unsalted butter, softened
2 cups sugar
4 large eggs, at room temperature
1½ cups self-rising flour
1¼ cups all-purpose flour
1 cup milk
1 teaspoon vanilla extract

MAKES 1 THREE-LAYER 9-INCH CAKE OR 24 CUPCAKES

Preheat oven to 350 degrees.

Grease and lightly flour three 9 x 2-inch round cake pans, then line the bottoms with waxed paper.

To make the cake: In a large bowl, on the medium speed of an electric mixer, cream the butter until smooth. Add the sugar gradually and beat until fluffy, about 3 minutes. Add the eggs one at a time, beating well after each addition. Combine the flours and add in four parts, alternating with the milk and the vanilla extract, beating well after each addition. Divide batter among the cake pans. Bake for 20–25 minutes or until a cake tester inserted into center of cake comes out clean. Let cakes cool in pans for ten minutes. Remove from pans and cool completely on wire rack.

If you're making cupcakes, line two 12-cup muffin tins with cupcake papers. Spoon the batter into the cups about three-quarters full. Bake until the tops spring back when lightly touched, about 20–22 minutes. Remove cupcakes from pans and cool completely on a rack before icing.

When cake has cooled, ice between the layers, then ice top and sides of cake.

Lemon Layer Cake

This moist and fluffy cake is equally delicious with Lemon Buttercream or Lemon Curd filling (recipes found on pages 85, 91).

1 cup (2 sticks) unsalted butter, softened
2 cups sugar
4 large eggs, at room temperature
1½ cups self-rising flour
1¼ cups all-purpose flour
¾ cup milk
¼ cup fresh lemon juice
2 teaspoons grated lemon zest

MAKES 1 THREE-LAYER 9-INCH CAKE

Preheat oven to 350 degrees.

Grease and lightly flour three 9 x 2-inch round cake pans, then line the bottoms with waxed paper.

To make the cake: In a large bowl, on the medium speed of an electric mixer, cream the butter until smooth. Add the sugar gradually and beat until fluffy, about 3 minutes. Add the eggs one at a time. Combine the flours and add in four parts, alternating with the milk and the lemon juice and zest, beating well after each addition. Divide the batter among the cake pans. Bake for 20–25 minutes or until a cake tester inserted into center of cake comes out clean. Let cakes cool in pans for 10 minutes. Remove from pans and cool completely on wire rack.

When cake has cooled, spread the icing or the curd evenly between layers and over top of cake.

Coconut Layer Cake

Allysa has had this recipe in her cookbook for years. It's originally from a woman named Kathy who lives in the Midwest. It's a wonderful cake and has become one of the all-time favorites among customers at the Magnolia Bakery. Kathy, we don't know you, but thanks a lot!

This cake is best served the day it is filled and frosted.

Cake

1 cup (2 sticks) unsalted butter, softened
2 cups sugar
4 large eggs, at room temperature
1½ cups self-rising flour
1¼ cups all-purpose flour
1 cup milk
1 teaspoon vanilla extract

Filling

¾ cup milk
½ cup sugar
2 tablespoons all-purpose flour
1 seven-ounce package sweetened, shredded coconut
1 teaspoon vanilla extract

Frosting:

3 egg whites
1½ teaspoons vanilla extract
½ cup cold water
1½ cups sugar
¼ plus ⅛ teaspoon cream of tartar

Preheat oven to 350 degrees.

Grease and lightly flour three 9 x 2-inch round cake pans, then line the bottoms with waxed paper.

To make the cake: In a large bowl, on the medium speed of an electric mixer, cream the butter until smooth. Add the sugar gradually and beat until fluffy, about 3 minutes. Add the eggs one at a time, beating well after each addition. Combine the flours and add in four parts, alternating with the milk and the vanilla extract, beating well after each addition. Divide the batter among the cake pans. Bake for 20–25 minutes or until a cake tester inserted into center of cake comes out clean. Let cakes cool in pans for 10 minutes. Remove from pans and cool completely on wire rack.

To make the filling: In a medium-size saucepan, whisk the milk with the sugar and the flour until thoroughly combined. Cook and stir constantly over medium-high heat (about 5 minutes) until thickened and bubbly. Remove from heat and add the coconut. Stir in the vanilla extract. Cover and cool to room temperature.

When cake has cooled, spread half the filling between the first two layers of cake, then the other half between the second and third layers. The cake should be assembled so it can be iced as soon as the frosting is completed.

To make the frosting: In an electric mixer bowl, combine the egg whites and the vanilla extract and set aside. In a medium-size saucepan over high heat, combine the water with the sugar and the cream of tartar. As mixture begins to bubble at edges, stir once to make sure the sugar is dissolved completely, then let come to a rolling boil (about 2–3 minutes) and remove immediately from heat.

Now, in a medium-size bowl, on the medium-high speed of an electric mixer, beat the egg whites and the vanilla extract with the whisk attachment until foamy, about 1 minute.

Without turning off mixer, pour the sugar syrup into the beaten egg whites in a thin, steady stream. Continue beating constantly, on medium-high speed, for about 5 minutes or until stiff peaks form but frosting is still creamy. Frost top and sides of cake immediately.

Generously sprinkle top with shredded coconut.

Garnish
Sweetened, shredded-coconut

MAKES 1 THREE-LAYER 9-INCH CAKE

Hummingbird Cake

This wonderful cake, filled with bananas, pineapples, and pecans, came our way by good fortune. One of our customers came into the bakery one afternoon with this recipe from his aunt, handwritten on an index card. He said she thought it would be a perfect cake for our bakery; she was right!

Cake
3 cups all-purpose flour
1 teaspoon cinnamon
1 teaspoon baking soda
1 teaspoon salt
1¼ cups vegetable oil
2 cups sugar
3 large eggs, at room temperature
1½ teaspoons vanilla extract
2 cups mashed, very ripe bananas
1 eight-ounce can crushed pineapple in unsweetened juice, drained (about 1 cup)
½ cup chopped pecans

Frosting
1 recipe Cream Cheese Icing (page 87)

Garnish
Coarsely chopped or whole pecans

Makes 1 two-layer 9-inch cake

Preheat oven to 325 degrees.

Grease and lightly flour two 9 x 2-inch round cake pans, then line the bottoms with waxed paper.

To make the cake: In a large bowl, sift together the flour, the cinnamon, the baking soda, and the salt. Set aside.

In a large bowl, on the medium speed of an electric mixer, beat the oil with the sugar until smooth, about 3 minutes. Add the eggs one at a time and beat until light, about 1 or 2 minutes. Add the vanilla extract. Add the bananas and the pineapple. Add the dry ingredients in thirds, beating after each addition until smooth. Stir in the pecans. Divide the batter between the prepared pans and bake for 40–50 minutes or until a cake tester inserted into center of cake comes out clean. Let cakes cool in pans for 10 minutes. Remove from pans and cool completely on wire rack.

When cake has cooled, ice between the layers, then ice top and sides of cake with our Cream Cheese Icing. Garnish with pecans as desired.

Apple Walnut Cake with Caramel Cream Cheese Icing

Caramel Pecan Brownies; Fudge Brownies with White Chocolate, Toffee, and Pecans; Peanut Butter Fudge Brownies; Raspberry Crumb Squares

Lemon Ice Box Pie

Oatmeal, Blueberry, and Corn Muffins

Aunt Daisy's Fresh Fruit Torte

Traditional Vanilla Birthday Cake cupcake with Traditional Vanilla Buttercream

Poppy Seed Coffee Cake

Coconut Layer Cake and Devil's Food Cake with Chocolate Buttercream

Here's a delicious twist on a vanilla cake Jennifer found in a vintage cookbook from 1954. The secret flavor is a hint of ginger. The frosting is a seven-minute icing made on the top of the stove. You must beat it continuously, but it's quick and easy, and the results are worth it!

Cake
3¾ cups self-rising flour
½ teaspoon ginger
¾ cup (1½ sticks) unsalted butter, softened
½ cup sugar
3 large eggs, at room temperature
1½ cups pure maple syrup
¾ cup hot water

Frosting
2 egg whites
½ cup maple syrup
¾ cup sugar
¼ teaspoon cream of tartar
¼ teaspoon salt
1 teaspoon vanilla extract
¼ teaspoon maple extract

Garnish
1 cup chopped walnuts

Makes 1 two-layer 9-inch cake

Preheat oven to 350 degrees.

Grease and lightly flour two 9 x 2-inch round cake pans, then line the bottoms with waxed paper.

To make the cake: In a large bowl, sift together the flour and the ginger and set aside.

In a large bowl, cream the butter and the sugar until fluffy, about 3 minutes. Add the eggs one at a time, beating until well combined. Beat in the maple syrup gradually. Add the flour mixture in thirds, alternating with the water, beating after each addition until smooth. Divide the batter between the prepared pans and bake for 30–35 minutes or until a cake tester inserted into center of cake comes out clean.

Let cakes cool in pans for 10 minutes. Remove from pans and cool completely on wire rack.

To make the frosting: In the top of a double boiler, combine first five ingredients. Cook over boiling water, beating constantly on the medium-high speed of an electric mixer, until mixture stands in peaks (about 5–7 minutes). Remove the pot from heat. Add the vanilla and the maple extracts and continue beating 1 minute more until thick enough to spread.

When cake has cooled, ice between the layers. Sprinkle about ⅓ cup chopped walnuts over the frosting. Then ice top and sides of cake, sprinkling the top with the remaining chopped walnuts.

Apple Walnut Cake with Caramel Cream Cheese Icing

We'd been making this exceptionally pretty cake for special orders only, but so many customers have requested it, it may soon become part of our standard cake repertoire. It's perfect for an autumn dinner party or as a delicious alternative to a Thanksgiving pie.

Cake

2 cups all-purpose flour
1 cup whole-wheat flour
1 teaspoon cinnamon
1 teaspoon baking soda
¾ teaspoon salt
1½ cups vegetable oil
2 cups sugar
3 large eggs, at room temperature
3 cups (3 large) golden Delicious apples, cut into 1-inch pieces
1 cup coarsely chopped walnuts
3 tablespoons apple-flavored brandy

Icing

1 pound (2 eight-ounce packages) cream cheese, softened slightly, cut into pieces
½ cup (1 stick) unsalted butter, softened slightly, cut into pieces
1 cup cold Caramel, plus extra (about ¼ cup) for decorating (recipe on page 92)

Garnish

Coarsely chopped or whole walnuts

Preheat oven to 325 degrees.

Grease and lightly flour two 9 x 2-inch round cake pans, then line the bottoms with waxed paper.

To make the cake: In a large bowl, sift together the flours, the cinnamon, the baking soda, and the salt. Set aside.

In a large bowl, on the medium speed of an electric mixer, beat the oil with the sugar until smooth, about 3 minutes. Add the eggs one at a time and beat until light, about 1 or 2 minutes. Add the dry ingredients in thirds, beating after each addition until smooth. The batter will be extremely thick and doughlike. With a spoon, stir in the apples, the walnuts, and the brandy until just blended. Divide the batter between the prepared pans and bake for 45–55 minutes or until a cake tester inserted into center of cake comes out clean. Let cakes cool in pans for 10 minutes. Remove from pans and cool completely on wire rack.

To make the icing: In a medium-size bowl, on the medium speed of an electric mixer, beat the cream cheese and the butter until smooth, about 3 minutes. Gradually add the Caramel and beat until well incorporated.

When cake has cooled, ice between the layers, then ice top and sides of cake. Drizzle remaining Caramel over top of cake, and using a small knife, swirl Caramel into icing, forming a decorative pattern. Garnish with walnuts as desired.

Makes 1 two-layer 9-inch cake

3/5/05 Cake tastes like a Devil Dog

Chocolate Buttermilk Layer Cake

We think this is the ideal chocolate layer cake. Moist and tender, this cake has a beautiful texture and a taste that's out of this world!

2 cups all-purpose flour
1 teaspoon baking soda
1 cup (2 sticks) unsalted butter, softened
1 cup sugar
1 cup firmly packed light brown sugar
4 large eggs, at room temperature
6 ounces unsweetened chocolate, melted (see Note)
1 cup buttermilk
1 teaspoon vanilla extract

Makes 1 two-layer 9-inch cake or 24 cupcakes

Preheat oven to 350 degrees.

Grease and lightly flour two 9 x 2-inch round cake pans, then line the bottoms with waxed paper.

In a medium-size bowl, sift together the flour and the baking soda. Set aside.

In a large bowl, cream the butter and the sugars until smooth, about 3 minutes. Add the eggs one at a time, beating well after each addition. Add the chocolate, mixing until well incorporated. Add the dry ingredients in thirds, alternating with the buttermilk and the vanilla extract, beating after each addition until smooth. Divide the batter between the prepared pans and bake for 25–35 minutes or until a cake tester inserted into center of cake comes out clean. Let cakes cool in pans for 10 minutes. Remove from pans and cool completely on wire racks.

If making cupcakes, line two 12-cup muffin tins with cupcake papers. Spoon the batter into the cups about three-quarters full. Bake until the tops spring back when lightly touched, about 20–22 minutes. Remove cupcakes from pans and cool on rack.

When cake has cooled, ice between the layers, then ice top and sides of cake. At the bakery we ice this cake with either Traditional Vanilla or Chocolate Buttercream (pages 83 or 84).

Note: To melt chocolate, place in a double boiler over simmering water on low heat for approximately 5–10 minutes. Stir occasionally until completely smooth and no pieces of chocolate remain. Remove from heat and let cool for 5–10 minutes.

Devil's Food Cake

At Allysa's house this cake was always iced with sweetened vanilla whipped cream. At the bakery we use a Mocha Buttercream (page 84). Whichever icing you choose, this devilishly rich chocolate cake is sure to be a hit.

3 cups all-purpose flour
1½ teaspoons baking powder
1½ teaspoons baking soda
¾ teaspoon salt
3 large eggs, separated, at room temperature (see first Note)
¾ cup (1½ sticks) unsalted butter, softened
2 cups firmly packed light brown sugar
8 ounces unsweetened chocolate, melted (see second Note)
2 cups milk
1½ teaspoons vanilla extract

Makes 1 two-layer 9-inch cake

Preheat oven to 350 degrees.

Grease and lightly flour two 9 x 2-inch round cake pans, then line the bottoms with waxed paper.

In a large bowl, sift together the flour, the baking powder, the baking soda, and the salt. Set aside.

Lightly beat the egg yolks until thick and lemon colored, about 2 minutes.

In a large bowl, cream the butter and the sugar until smooth, about 3 minutes. Add the egg yolks, beating until well combined. Add the chocolate, mixing until well incorporated. Add the dry ingredients in thirds, alternating with the milk and the vanilla extract, beating after each addition until smooth. In a separate bowl, beat the egg whites on the high speed of an electric mixer until soft peaks form. Gently fold into the batter. Divide the batter between the prepared pans and bake for 40–45 minutes or until a cake tester inserted into center of cake comes out clean. Let cakes cool in pans for 10 minutes. Remove from pans and cool completely on wire racks. When cake has cooled, ice between the layers, then ice top and sides of cake.

Note: It is best to separate the eggs when cold and then allow them to come to room temperature before proceeding with the recipe.

Note: To melt chocolate, place in a double boiler over simmering water on low heat for approximately 5–10 minutes. Stir occasionally until completely smooth and no pieces of chocolate remain. Remove from heat and let cool for 5–10 minutes.

German Chocolate Cake

We confess we've improved on a classic recipe. Baker's German's Sweet Chocolate is the chocolate of choice for this cake.

Cake
1 package (4 ounces) Baker's German's Sweet Chocolate, broken into squares
½ cup water
2 cups all-purpose flour
1½ teaspoons baking soda
¼ teaspoon salt
4 large eggs, separated, at room temperature (see Note)
1 cup (2 sticks) unsalted butter, softened
2 cups sugar
1 teaspoon vanilla extract
1 cup buttermilk

Caramel Pecan Filling and Frosting:
1½ cans (18 ounces) evaporated milk
6 egg yolks
2 cups sugar
1 cup (2 sticks) unsalted butter, cut into small pieces
2 teaspoons vanilla extract
4 cups sweetened, shredded coconut
2 cups coarsely chopped pecans

Makes 1 three-layer 9-inch cake

Preheat oven to 350 degrees.

Grease and lightly flour three 9 x 2-inch round cake pans, then line the bottoms with waxed paper.

To make the cake: In a small saucepan over low heat, combine the chocolate with the water, stirring to melt the chocolate, and blend well. Set aside to cool for 10 minutes.

Meanwhile, in a medium-size bowl, sift together the flour, the baking soda, and the salt. Set aside.

In a small bowl, lightly beat the egg yolks, about 1 minute.

In a large bowl, on the medium speed of an electric mixer, cream the butter and the sugar until light and fluffy, about 3 minutes. Add the egg yolks, beating until well combined. Add the chocolate mixture and the vanilla extract. Add the dry ingredients in thirds, alternating with the buttermilk, beating after each addition, until smooth. In a separate bowl, beat the egg whites on the high speed of an electric mixer until soft peaks form. Gently fold into batter. Divide batter among the prepared pans. Bake for 25–30 minutes or until a cake tester inserted into center of cake comes out clean. Be careful not to overbake, as this cake has a different, lighter texture than most.

Let cake cool in pans for 10 minutes. Remove from pans and cool completely on wire rack.

To make the frosting: In a large saucepan, beat together the evaporated milk and the egg yolks. Stir in the sugar, the butter, and the vanilla extract. Stir over medium heat about 15–18 minutes or until thickened and bubbly and golden in color. Remove from heat. Stir in the coconut and the pecans. Transfer to a large bowl and cool until room temperature and of good spreading consistency (about 2 hours; frosting will thicken as it cools).

When cake has cooled, spread frosting between layers and over top of cake.

Note: It is best to separate the eggs when cold and then allow them to come to room temperature before proceeding with the recipe.

Other Cakes

Lemon Vanilla Bundt Cake

Jennifer's mom, Susanne, developed this pound cake recipe about fifteen years ago. It's a surefire hit every time it's served, and there's never an Appel get-together without it. The secret to the tender crumb is the club soda. Kudos to Mom!

1½ cups (3 sticks) unsalted butter, softened
3 cups sugar
5 large eggs, at room temperature
3 cups all-purpose flour
¾ cup club soda (not *seltzer)*
2 tablespoons vanilla extract
1½ tablespoons grated lemon zest

Makes one 10-inch cake

Preheat oven to 350 degrees.

Grease and lightly flour a 10-inch Bundt pan.

In a large bowl, on the medium speed of an electric mixer, cream the butter and the sugar until fluffy, about 3 minutes. Add the eggs one at a time, mixing well after each addition. Add the flour in thirds, alternating with the club soda, beating after each addition until smooth. Add the vanilla extract and the lemon zest and mix well. Pour the batter into prepared pan and bake 70–80 minutes until golden brown or a cake tester inserted into center of cake comes out clean. Let cake cool in pan for 20 minutes. Remove from pan and cool completely on wire rack.

Variation: For an equally delicious cake, try this as a marble cake. Pour ⅔ of the batter into prepared pan, then pour ⅓ cup unsweetened cocoa powder on top. Gently press the powder down into the batter with a large spoon. Pour in the remaining batter. Baking time should remain the same.

Chocolate Amaretto Bundt Cake

After tasting a delicious cake at another bakery, Jennifer was so impressed that she developed this recipe from scratch to try to match their confection. We think you'll love this unbelievably moist and chocolaty cake.

2 cups all-purpose flour
1 teaspoon baking soda
1 cup (2 sticks) unsalted butter, softened
1 cup sugar
1 cup firmly packed light brown sugar
4 large eggs, at room temperature
6 ounces semisweet chocolate, melted (see Note)
1 cup milk
3 teaspoons almond extract
1 teaspoon vanilla extract
4 tablespoons amaretto-flavored liqueur

MAKES ONE 10-INCH CAKE

Preheat oven to 350 degrees.

Grease and lightly flour a 10-inch Bundt pan.

In a medium-size bowl, sift together the flour and the baking soda. Set aside.

In a large bowl, on the medium speed of an electric mixer, cream the butter and the sugars until fluffy, about 3 minutes. Add the eggs one at a time, mixing well after each addition. Add the chocolate, mixing until well incorporated. Add the dry ingredients in thirds, alternating with the milk and the extracts, beating after each addition until smooth. Add the liqueur and mix well. Pour the batter into prepared pan and bake 45–50 minutes or until a cake tester inserted into center of cake comes out clean. Let cake cool in pan for 20 minutes. Remove from pan and cool completely on wire rack.

NOTE: To melt chocolate, place in a double boiler over simmering water on low heat for approximately 5–10 minutes. Stir occasionally until completely smooth and no pieces of chocolate remain. Remove from heat and let cool for 5–10 minutes.

Chocolate Sour Cream Cake with Chocolate Chips

This simple but chocolaty cake has a nice sour cream tang to it. It's the kind of cake that sits on the kitchen table to be shared with visiting neighbors over a cup of coffee.

3 cups plus 2 tablespoons all-purpose flour
1½ teaspoons baking soda
¼ teaspoon salt
3 ounces unsweetened chocolate, coarsely chopped
1 tablespoon instant espresso
1½ cups boiling water
¾ cup (1½ sticks) unsalted butter, softened
2⅔ cups firmly packed light brown sugar
2 large eggs, at room temperature
1½ teaspoons vanilla extract
¾ cup sour cream
⅔ cup miniature chocolate chips

Makes one 10-inch cake

Preheat oven to 325 degrees.

Grease and lightly flour a 10-inch tube pan.

In a large bowl, sift together the flour, the baking soda, and the salt. Set aside.

Place the chocolate and the espresso in a medium-size bowl. Add the boiling water and stir until chocolate is melted. Set aside to cool for 5 or 10 minutes.

Meanwhile, in a large bowl, on the low speed of an electric mixer, cream the butter with the sugar until fluffy, about 3 minutes. Add the eggs one at at time, beating well after each addition. Add the vanilla extract. Gradually add the dry ingredients, beating only until smooth. Add the sour cream. Add the chocolate mixture in three parts, beating after each addition. Stir in the chocolate chips. Pour the batter into prepared pan and bake for 70–80 minutes or until a cake tester inserted into center of cake comes out clean.

Let cake cool in pan for 20 minutes. Remove from pan and cool completely on wire rack.

Poppy Seed Coffee Cake

Despite the belief of many New Yorkers, poppy seeds aren't found just on bagels. Try this yummy and unique version of an old standby the next time the folks pop in for coffee and cake. As a variation, try using prune or apricot filling in place of the poppy filling.

Coffee Cake

1½ cups all-purpose flour
1 teaspoon baking powder
¼ teaspoon salt
2 eggs, separated, at room temperature (see Note)
½ cup solid vegetable shortening
½ cup sugar
½ cup milk
1 twelve-ounce can poppy filling

Topping

6 tablespoons all-purpose flour
¼ cup brown sugar
½ teaspoon baking powder
2 tablespoons unsalted butter, softened

Makes 1 cake

Preheat oven to 350 degrees.

Line an 8 x 8 x 2-inch square baking pan with waxed paper.

To prepare the coffee cake: In a medium-size bowl, sift together the flour, the baking powder, and the salt. Set aside.

In a small bowl, lightly beat the egg yolks, about 1 minute.

In a large bowl, on the low speed of an electric mixer, cream the shortening and the sugar until fluffy, about 2–3 minutes. Add the egg yolks. Add the dry ingredients in two parts, alternating with the milk. In a separate bowl, on the high speed of an electric mixer, beat the egg whites until stiff peaks form. Gently fold the egg whites into the batter. Batter will be thick and doughlike.

Meanwhile, prepare the topping: In a small bowl, mix together the flour, the brown sugar, and the baking powder. Using a pastry blender, cut in the butter until the mixture resembles coarse crumbs.

Pour the batter into prepared pan. Make indentations with the back of a spoon and press teaspoonfuls of the poppy filling into each indentation. Sprinkle the topping over cake. Bake 40–45 minutes or until a cake tester comes out with moist crumbs attached. Do not overbake.

Allow to cool for 20 minutes before cutting and serving.

Note: It is best to separate the eggs when cold and then allow them to come to room temperature before proceeding with the recipe.

Dump Cake

Upon hearing that we were collecting recipes for our cookbook, customer Steven Kaplan, who is from the South, told us of a wonderful dessert his mom always made, called "dump cake." "It's the easiest thing in the world," says Kaplan, "because you just dump in all the ingredients, and out comes this terrific cake!" He sure was right!

1 twenty-one-ounce can cherry pie filling
1 sixteen-ounce can crushed pineapple, with juice
½ box white cake mix (just the plain mix, nothing added)
1½ cups coarsely chopped pecans
½ cup (1 stick) unsalted butter, cut into thin slices

Preheat oven to 325 degrees.

Pour the cherry pie filling into a 13 x 9-inch glass baking dish and smooth evenly over the bottom of dish with a rubber spatula. Pour canned pineapple over the pie filling. Sprinkle the white cake mix completely over the pineapple. Place pecans evenly over cake mix. Top with slices of butter. Bake about 45 minutes or until cake appears golden brown and bubbly. Serve warm right from the dish with a dollop of whipped cream.

MAKES 1 CAKE

This recipe was handed down to our friend Debra Davis from her Texan grandmother, Winifred Crawford. The cake can also be made with red or golden Delicious apples and with or without the glaze. You won't be disappointed with any variation.

Cake
3 cups all-purpose flour
2 cups sugar
½ teaspoon baking soda
½ teaspoon salt
1 cup plus 2 tablespoons vegetable oil
3 large eggs, at room temperature
1 teaspoon vanilla extract
2 Bosc pears, cut into 1-inch pieces (about 2 cups)
1 cup coarsely chopped pecans

Glaze
1½ cups confectioners' sugar
3 tablespoons water

MAKES ONE 10-INCH CAKE

Preheat oven to 350 degrees.

Lightly grease a 10-inch tube pan.

To make the cake: In a large bowl, sift together the flour, the sugar, the baking soda, and the salt, making a well in the center. Stir in the oil, the eggs, and the vanilla extract. Stir in the pears and the pecans. Spoon the batter into prepared pan. Bake for 60–70 minutes or until a cake tester inserted into center of cake comes out clean. Let cake cool in pan for 20 minutes. Remove from pan and cool completely on wire rack.

To make the glaze: In a small bowl, stir together the sugar and the water until smooth. Drizzle decoratively over cooled cake. Garnish with pecans if desired.

Here's a quick and easy confection that lends itself to any fruit combination you might desire. We decided to use pears and cranberries for a delicious autumn torte.

½ cup (1 stick) unsalted butter, softened
1 cup sugar
2 large eggs, at room temperature
1 cup all-purpose flour
1 teaspoon baking powder
1 teaspoon vanilla extract
1 Bosc pear, thinly sliced (about 1 cup)
½ cup cranberries, coarsely chopped
1 tablespoon cinnamon sugar

MAKES 1 NINE-INCH TORTE

Preheat oven to 350 degrees.

Grease and lightly flour one 9 x 2-inch round cake pan, then line the bottom with waxed paper.

In a large bowl, on the low speed of an electric mixer, cream the butter and the sugar until fluffy, about 3 minutes. Add the eggs one at a time, beating well after each addition. Add the flour, the baking powder, and the vanilla extract until well incorporated. Pour the batter into prepared pan. Spread the pear slices and the berries evenly over the batter. Sprinkle with cinnamon sugar. Bake for about 1 hour until golden brown. Serve warm with a dollop of whipped cream, if desired.

Icings, Fillings, and Frostings

Traditional Vanilla Buttercream

Customers at the bakery have been begging us for the secret to our Vanilla Buttercream recipe since we opened our doors. This simple confectioners' sugar icing's "secret" is that we just whip it longer than you'd think necessary to get that extra-creamy texture.

1 cup (2 sticks) unsalted butter, very soft
8 cups confectioners' sugar
½ cup milk
2 teaspoons vanilla extract

Place the butter in a large mixing bowl. Add 4 cups of the sugar and then the milk and the vanilla extract. Beat until smooth and creamy. Gradually add the remaining sugar, 1 cup at a time, until icing is thick enough to be of good spreading consistency (you may very well not need all of the sugar). If desired, add a few drops of food coloring and mix thoroughly. Use and store icing at room temperature, as icing will set if chilled. Can store in airtight container up to three days.

THIS YIELDS ICING FOR 1 TWO- OR THREE-LAYER 9-INCH CAKE OR 24 CUPCAKES

Chocolate Buttercream

1 cup (2 sticks) unsalted butter, very soft
1 tablespoon plus 1 teaspoon milk
6 ounces semisweet chocolate, melted and cooled to lukewarm (see Note)
1 teaspoon vanilla extract
1¼ cups sifted *confectioners' sugar*

THIS YIELDS ICING FOR 1 TWO- OR THREE-LAYER 9-INCH CAKE OR 24 CUPCAKES

In a medium-size bowl, beat the butter until creamy, about 3 minutes. Add the milk carefully and beat until smooth. Add the melted chocolate and beat well. Add the vanilla extract and beat for 3 minutes. Gradually add the sugar and beat until creamy and of desired consistency.

NOTE: To melt chocolate, place in a double boiler over simmering water on low heat for approximately 5–10 minutes. Stir occasionally until completely smooth and no pieces of chocolate remain. Remove from heat and let cool for 5–10 minutes.

VARIATION: Mocha Buttercream. Add 2–3 teaspoons instant espresso powder after adding the sugar and continue with the recipe.

Lemon Buttercream

1 cup (2 sticks) unsalted butter, very soft
8 cups confectioners' sugar
½ cup fresh lemon juice
1 teaspoon grated lemon zest

THIS YIELDS ICING FOR 1 TWO- OR THREE-LAYER 9-INCH CAKE

Place the butter in a large mixing bowl. Add 4 cups of the sugar and then the juice and the zest. Beat until smooth and creamy. Gradually add the remaining sugar, 1 cup at at time, until icing is thick enough to be of good spreading consistency. If desired, add a few drops of yellow food coloring and mix thoroughly. Use and store at room temperature.

Seven-Minute Icing

Seven-Minute Icing is a cooked frosting, but it is not made with a sugar syrup and so does not require the use of a candy thermometer. It is relatively simple to make and can be used to ice a wide variety of cakes. We especially love it on the Old-Fashioned White Cake (page 59) or the Devil's Food Cake (page 68).

3 egg whites
2¼ cups sugar
½ cup cold water
1½ tablespoons light corn syrup
⅛ teaspoon salt
1½ teaspoons vanilla extract

THIS YIELDS ICING FOR 1 TWO- OR THREE-LAYER 9-INCH CAKE

In the top of a double boiler, combine the first five ingredients and place over rapidly boiling water. On the high speed of an electric mixer, beat constantly for 6–8 minutes or until icing stands up in soft peaks. Remove from heat, add the vanilla extract, and beat about 1 minute more or until of desired spreading consistency. Use immediately.

Cream Cheese Icing

A not-too-sweet icing option for a variety of layer cakes, though especially suited to the Hummingbird Cake (page 64). This icing could also be used on our Poppy Seed Bread (page 29) or Pear Pecan Cake (page 78).

1 pound (2 eight-ounce packages) cream cheese, softened slightly, cut into small pieces
½ cup (1 stick) unsalted butter, softened slightly, cut into small pieces
1½ teaspoons vanilla extract
5 cups sifted *confectioners' sugar*

In a medium-size bowl, on the medium speed of an electric mixer, beat the cream cheese and the butter until smooth, about 3 minutes. Add the vanilla extract. Gradually add the sugar and beat until well incorporated.

THIS YIELDS ICING FOR 1 TWO- OR THREE-LAYER 9-INCH CAKE

Chocolate Glaze

A simple glaze (or ganache) that is great to pour over any desired dessert; we suggest it over our Chocolate Sour Cream Cake with Chocolate Chips (page 75), or our Chocolate Amaretto Bundt Cake (page 74).

4 ounces semisweet chocolate
4 tablespoons butter or cream
1–2 tablespoons liquor or liqueur of your choice (Bourbon, rum, Grand Marnier, amaretto, brandy, and so on)

THIS YIELDS ENOUGH GLAZE TO COVER ONE 10-INCH TUBE OR BUNDT CAKE

In a medium-size saucepan over low heat, melt the chocolate and the butter, stirring occasionally until completely melted. Remove from heat and stir in desired liquor. Use immediately over completely cooled dessert. Allow to set for 15 minutes. Can be refrigerated and reheated gently if necessary.

This is a classic custard. It's fantastic in cakes as a filling or as a dessert accompanied by a simple cookie.

1 cup sugar
6 tablespoons all-purpose flour
¼ teaspoon salt
2 cups milk
4 egg yolks, slightly beaten
1 tablespoon plus 1 teaspoon vanilla extract

THIS YIELDS FILLING FOR 1 TWO- OR THREE-LAYER 9-INCH CAKE

In a small bowl, combine the sugar, the flour, and the salt. Set aside.

In a heavy-bottomed medium-size saucepan, heat the milk until very hot but not boiling. Remove from heat. Pour the milk into the dry ingredients and beat until well blended. Pour back into pot and stir continuously over low heat for 5 minutes until very thick and smooth. Add the egg yolks and cook for 3 more minutes. Remove from heat and cool for 10 minutes, stirring from time to time. Then add the vanilla extract. Cover and refrigerate until needed.

Butterscotch Filling

This rich custard has a distinctive caramel flavor. It's especially good with white or yellow cake.

1 cup firmly packed dark brown sugar
4 tablespoons (½ stick) unsalted butter
2 cups milk
6 tablespoons all-purpose flour
1 teaspoon salt
4 large eggs, slightly beaten
1 teaspoon vanilla extract

THIS YIELDS FILLING FOR 1 TWO- OR THREE-LAYER 9-INCH CAKE

In a heavy-bottomed medium-size saucepan, combine the sugar and the butter, cooking over low heat. Stir constantly until the sugar has melted and the mixture is thoroughly blended. Add 1 cup of the milk, blend well, and continue cooking over low heat. In a small bowl, combine the flour and the salt with the remaining cup of milk and beat until smooth. Add this to the first mixture, stirring or whisking constantly. Continue cooking until thickened. Beat in the eggs and cook another 2 minutes. Remove from heat and cool for 10 minutes, stirring from time to time. Then add the vanilla extract. Cover and refrigerate until needed.

Lemon Curd Filling

Try this on toast or scones for a sweet breakfast or teatime treat.

12 egg yolks, at room temperature
3 tablespoons grated lemon zest
1 cup fresh lemon juice
½ teaspoon lemon extract
1½ cups sugar
1 cup (2 sticks) unsalted butter, cut in small pieces

In a medium-size saucepan, whisk in the first five ingredients until thoroughly combined. Using a wooden spoon, stir constantly over medium heat. Cook about 20 minutes until thick and bubbly. Remove from heat and add the butter, one piece at a time, stirring to incorporate. Place in refrigerator overnight until firm.

MAKES 3½ CUPS, OR ENOUGH FILLING FOR 1 TWO- OR THREE-LAYER 9-INCH CAKE

This is a little tricky, but worth the time and trouble. Be careful when adding the cream to the sugar syrup; it may splatter.

1 cup cold water
3 cups sugar
2 cups heavy cream, at room temperature

MAKES 3½ CUPS

In a medium-size saucepan, combine the water and the sugar. Set over medium-low heat, stirring occasionally, until the sugar dissolves (about 3 minutes), making sure no sugar is sticking to sides of pan. Increase heat to high and boil without stirring, until the syrup becomes a deep amber color, about 15 minutes. To prevent the syrup from becoming grainy, use a pastry brush dipped into cold water to brush down any sugar crystals sticking to the sides of the pan. Swirl the pan occasionally for even browning.

Once the syrup turns deep amber in color, immediately remove from heat. Slowly and carefully add the cream to the syrup (mixture will bubble vigorously), whisking constantly, until cream is incorporated.

Return the pan to medium-low heat, stirring until sauce is smooth, about 1 minute.

Remove from heat and allow to come to room temperature before refrigerating. Can be stored for up to one month in refrigerator.

Cheesecakes

When Allysa was growing up, her dad would rave about a fabulous crumb-topped cheesecake he enjoyed as a child in Brooklyn but had never seen since. After some experimenting, she came up with this recipe, unique in that it's made without a crust (but we believe you'll agree that the confectioners' sugar topping, with a hint of cinnamon, more than makes up for it).

Filling

2 pounds (4 eight-ounce packages) cream cheese, softened
1¼ cups sugar
5 large eggs, at room temperature
2 tablespoons heavy cream
1 tablespoon vanilla extract

Topping

2 cups all-purpose flour
2 cups confectioners' sugar
½ teaspoon cinnamon
1½ teaspoons baking powder
1 cup (2 sticks) unsalted butter, cut into small pieces

Makes one 10-inch cheesecake

Preheat oven to 325 degrees. Butter the bottom and sides of a 10-inch springform pan.

To make the filling: In a large bowl, on the low speed of an electric mixer, beat the cream cheese until very smooth. Gradually add the sugar. Add the eggs one at a time. To ensure that the batter has no lumps and that no ingredients are stuck to the bottom of the bowl, stop the mixer several times and scrape down the sides of the bowl with a rubber spatula. Stir in the heavy cream and the vanilla extract.

Pour the batter into the prepared pan and set the pan on a baking sheet. Bake for 40 minutes.

Meanwhile, prepare the topping: In a medium-size bowl, mix together the flour, the sugar, the cinnamon, and the baking powder. Using a pastry blender, cut in the butter until the mixture resembles coarse crumbs.

Slowly and carefully remove cheesecake, with baking sheet, to add topping. Sprinkle crumbs evenly over top of cake, return it immediately to oven, and bake for an additional 20 minutes.

Bake until edges are set and center moves only slightly when pan is shaken, about 1 hour. At the end of the baking time, turn off the heat, and using a wooden spoon to keep oven door slightly ajar, cool cake in oven for 1 hour before removing. Cover and refrigerate for at least 12 hours.

Remove cake from the refrigerator at least 15–30 minutes before cutting and serving.

The secret to the success of this cheesecake is the homemade caramel mixed with the nutty flavor of the toasted pecans. At our bakery it's a sure sell-out every time.

Crust
½ cup (1 stick) unsalted butter, melted
1¼ cup vanilla wafer crumbs
½ cup finely chopped pecans

Filling
2 pounds (4 eight-ounce packages) cream cheese, softened
1¼ cups sugar
5 large eggs, at room temperature
2 tablespoons heavy cream
1 tablespoon vanilla extract

Topping
1 cup cold Caramel (or more if desired) (recipe on page 92)
1 cup coarsely chopped toasted pecans (see Note)

MAKE ONE 10-INCH CHEESECAKE

Preheat oven to 325 degrees.

To make the crust: In a small bowl, combine the butter with the vanilla wafer crumbs and the pecans. Press into the bottom of a buttered 10-inch springform pan. Bake for 10 minutes. Remove from oven and cool on rack.

To make the filling: In a large bowl, on the low speed of an electric mixer, beat the cream cheese until very smooth. Gradually add the sugar. Add the eggs one at a time. To ensure that the batter has no lumps and that no ingredients are stuck to the bottom of the bowl, stop the mixer several times and scrape down the sides of the bowl with a rubber spatula. Stir in the heavy cream and the vanilla extract.

Pour the batter into the prepared pan and set the pan on a baking sheet. Bake until edges are set and center moves only slightly when pan is shaken, about 1 hour. At the end of the baking time, turn off the heat, and using a wooden spoon to keep oven door slightly ajar, cool cake in oven for 1 hour before removing. Cover and refrigerate for at least 12 hours.

Spoon cold Caramel evenly over top of cake. Sprinkle with pecans. Return cake to refrigerator.

Remove cake from the refrigerator at least 15–30 minutes before cutting and serving.

NOTE: To toast pecans, place on a baking sheet in a 325-degree oven for approximately 10–15 minutes or until lightly browned and fragrant.

This unbelievably delicious cheesecake will have toffee lovers clamoring for seconds; now, you can have your cake and candy, too. Allysa, who feels that the addition of Heath Bars to just about any dessert is a good thing, developed this idea one rare quiet evening at the bakery.

Crust
1 cup all-purpose flour
¼ cup confectioners' sugar
1 cup finely chopped toasted almonds (see Note)
½ cup (1 stick) unsalted butter, softened, cut into small pieces

Filling
2 pounds (4 eight-ounce packages) cream cheese, softened
1¼ cups sugar
5 large eggs, at room temperature
2 tablespoons heavy cream
1 tablespoon vanilla extract

Topping
3 coarsely chopped Heath Bars or chocolate-covered toffee bars (about ¾ cup)
¾ cup coarsely chopped toasted almonds (see Note)

Makes one 10-inch cheesecake

Preheat oven to 325 degrees.

To make the crust: In a medium-size bowl, combine the flour with the sugar and the almonds. Using a pastry blender, cut in the butter until the mixture resembles coarse crumbs. Press into the bottom of a buttered 10-inch springform pan. Bake for 10 minutes. Remove from oven and cool on rack.

To make the filling: In a large bowl, on the low speed of an electric mixer, beat the cream cheese until very smooth. Gradually add the sugar. Add the eggs one at a time. To ensure that the batter has no lumps and that no ingredients are stuck to the bottom of the bowl, stop the mixer several times and scrape down the sides of the bowl with a rubber spatula. Stir in the heavy cream and the vanilla extract.

Pour the batter into the prepared pan and set the pan on a baking sheet. Bake until edges are set and center moves only slightly when pan is shaken, about 1 hour. At the end of the baking time, remove cheesecake from oven to add topping. Sprinkle Heath Bars and almonds evenly over top of cake and return to oven to cool. Turn off the heat, and using a wooden spoon to keep oven door slightly ajar, cool cake in oven for 1 hour before removing. Cover and refrigerate for at least 12 hours.

Remove cake from the refrigerator at least 15–30 minutes before cutting and serving.

Note: To toast almonds, place on a baking sheet in a 325-degree oven for approximately 10–15 minutes or until lightly browned and fragrant.

With a crunchy chocolate almond crust and topping sandwiching a chocolaty-smooth and creamy filling, this cheesecake is a multitextured masterpiece!

Crust
6 tablespoons (¾ stick) unsalted butter, melted
1½ cups chocolate-sandwich cookie crumbs
½ cup finely chopped toasted almonds (see second Note)

Filling
1 pound (2 eight-ounce packages) cream cheese, softened
4 ounces almond paste, crumbled
1 cup sugar
3 large eggs, at room temperature
6 ounces semisweet chocolate, melted (see first Note)
1½ teaspoons vanilla extract
5 tablespoons amaretto-flavored liqueur
3 cups sour cream, at room temperature

Preheat oven to 325 degrees.

To make the crust: In a small bowl, combine the butter with the chocolate cookie crumbs and the almonds. Press into the bottom of a buttered 10-inch springform pan. Bake for 10 minutes. Remove from oven and cool on rack.

To make the filling: In a large bowl, on the low speed of an electric mixer, beat the cream cheese and the almond paste until very smooth. Gradually add the sugar. Add the eggs one at a time. To ensure that the batter has no lumps and that no ingredients are stuck to the bottom of the bowl, stop the mixer several times and scrape down the sides of the bowl with a rubber spatula. Beat in the melted chocolate until smooth. Stir in the vanilla extract and the liqueur until well combined. Then stir in the sour cream, mixing thoroughly.

Pour the batter into the prepared pan and set the pan on a baking sheet. Bake until edges are set and center moves only slightly when pan is shaken, about 80 minutes. At the end of the baking time, remove cheesecake from oven to add topping. Sprinkle cookie crumbs and almonds evenly over top of cake, and return to oven to cool.

Turn off the heat, and using a wooden spoon to keep oven door slightly ajar, cool the cake in oven for 1 hour before removing. Cover and refrigerate for at least 12 hours.

Remove cake from the refrigerator at least 15–30 minutes before cutting and serving.

Note: To melt chocolate, place in a double boiler over simmering water on low heat for approximately 5–10 minutes. Stir occasionally until completely smooth and no pieces of chocolate remain. Remove from heat and let cool for 5–10 minutes.

Note: To toast almonds, place on a baking sheet in a 325-degree oven for approximately 10–15 minutes or until lightly browned and fragrant.

Topping

½ cup crumbled chocolate-sandwich cookies

½ cup coarsely chopped toasted almonds (see second Note)

Makes one 10-inch cheesecake

Chocolate Swirl Cheesecake

For those who like a subtle touch of chocolate, this is the cheesecake for you! One of our original cheesecakes, it's still a big favorite at the bakery.

Crust

5 tablespoons unsalted butter, melted

2 cups chocolate wafer crumbs

Filling

2 pounds (4 eight-ounce packages) cream cheese, softened

1¼ cups sugar

5 large eggs, at room temperature

2 tablespoons heavy cream

1 tablespoon vanilla extract

Topping

3 tablespoons heavy cream

4 ounces semisweet chocolate, finely chopped

MAKES ONE 10-INCH CHEESECAKE

Preheat oven to 325 degrees.

To make the crust: In a small bowl, combine the butter with the chocolate wafer crumbs. Press into the bottom of a buttered 10-inch springform pan. Bake for 10 minutes. Remove from oven and cool on rack.

To make the filling: In a large bowl, on the low speed of an electric mixer, beat the cream cheese until very smooth. Gradually add the sugar. Add the eggs one at a time. To ensure that the batter has no lumps and that no ingredients are stuck to the bottom of the bowl, stop the mixer several times, and scrape down the sides of the bowl with a rubber spatula. Stir in the heavy cream and the vanilla extract.

Pour the batter into the prepared pan and set the pan on a baking sheet.

To prepare the topping: In a small saucepan over high heat, bring the heavy cream to a simmer. Add the chocolate, turning heat down to low and stirring constantly until chocolate is completely melted. Remove from heat and cool slightly. Drop this mixture by the teaspoonful onto top of batter. Using the tip of a sharp knife, swirl chocolate mixture into batter, forming a decorative pattern.

Bake until edges are set and center moves only slightly when pan is shaken, about 1 hour. At the end of the baking time, turn off the heat, and using a wooden spoon to keep oven door slightly ajar, cool cake in oven for 1 hour before removing. Cover and refrigerate for at least 12 hours.

Remove cake from the refrigerator at least 15–30 minutes before cutting and serving.

White Chocolate Hazelnut Cheesecake

Allysa and her cousin Kim brainstormed one Thanksgiving when an uneven oven produced a cheesecake with cracks on the surface. They decided to pile white chocolate and nuts on top to cover up the cracks and created a cake that turned out to be more delicious than the original.

Crust
½ cup (1 stick) unsalted butter, melted
1 cup graham cracker crumbs
¼ cup sugar
½ cup ground toasted hazelnuts (see Note)

Filling
2 pounds (4 eight-ounce packages) cream cheese, softened
1¼ cups sugar
4 large eggs, at room temperature
3 ounces white chocolate, finely chopped
3 tablespoons Frangelico liqueur

Topping
1 cup coarsely chopped toasted hazelnuts (see Note)
1 cup coarsely chopped white chocolate

Preheat oven to 325 degrees.

To make the crust: In a small bowl, combine the butter with the graham cracker crumbs, the sugar, and the hazelnuts. Press into the bottom of a buttered 10-inch springform pan. Bake for 10 minutes. Remove from oven and cool on rack.

To make the filling: In a large bowl, on the low speed of an electric mixer, beat the cream cheese until very smooth. Gradually add the sugar. Add the eggs one at a time. To ensure that the batter has no lumps and that no ingredients are stuck to the bottom of the bowl, stop the mixer several times, and scrape down the sides of the bowl with a rubber spatula. Stir in the white chocolate and the liqueur until well combined.

Pour the batter into the prepared pan and set the pan on a baking sheet. After 40 minutes, carefully remove from oven and sprinkle hazelnuts and white chocolate evenly over top of cake. Return immediately to oven and bake an additional 20 minutes, until edges are set and center moves only slightly when pan is shaken. At the end of the baking time, turn off the heat, and using a wooden spoon to keep oven door slightly ajar, cool cake in oven for 1 hour before removing. Cover and refrigerate for at least 12 hours.

Remove cake from the refrigerator at least 15–30 minutes before cutting and serving.

NOTE: To toast hazelnuts, place on a baking sheet in a 325-degree oven for approximately 10–15 minutes or until lightly browned and fragrant.

MAKES ONE 10-INCH CHEESECAKE

Mocha Rum Cheesecake

The rum, espresso, and chocolaty-creamy filling atop a dark chocolate cookie crust makes this cheesecake pure decadence.

Crust

4 tablespoons (½ stick) unsalted butter, melted
1½ cups chocolate wafer crumbs

Filling

4 tablespoons light rum
1 tablespoon instant espresso
1 pound (2 eight-ounce packages) cream cheese, softened
1 cup sugar
3 large eggs, at room temperature
4 ounces semisweet chocolate, melted (see Note)
1½ teaspoons vanilla extract
3 cups sour cream, at room temperature

Makes one 10-inch cheesecake

Preheat oven to 325 degrees.

To make the crust: In a small bowl, combine the butter with the chocolate wafer crumbs. Press into the bottom of a buttered 10-inch springform pan. Bake for 10 minutes. Remove from oven and cool on rack.

To make the filling: In a separate bowl, whisk the rum and the espresso until well blended. Set aside.

In a large bowl, on the low speed of an electric mixer, beat the cream cheese until very smooth. Gradually add the sugar. Add the eggs one at a time. To ensure that the batter has no lumps and that no ingredients are stuck to the bottom of the bowl, stop the mixer several times and scrape down the sides of the bowl with a rubber spatula. Beat in the melted chocolate until smooth. Stir in the vanilla extract and the rum mixture until well combined. Stir in the sour cream, mixing thoroughly.

Pour the batter into the prepared pan and set the pan on a baking sheet. Bake until edges are set and center moves only slightly when pan is shaken, about 80 minutes. At the end of the baking time, turn off the heat, and using a wooden spoon to keep oven door slightly ajar, cool the cake in oven for 1 hour before removing. Cover and refrigerate for at least 12 hours.

Remove cake from the refrigerator at least 15–30 minutes before cutting and serving.

Note: To melt chocolate, place in a double boiler over simmering water on low heat for approximately 5–10 minutes. Stir occasionally until completely smooth, and no pieces of chocolate remain. Remove from heat and let cool for 5–10 minutes.

Raspberry Marzipan Cheesecake

Growing up with German grandparents, Jennifer often received marzipan as a treat. It remains one of her favorite sweets to this day and incorporated into this cheesecake makes this a delectable dessert.

Crust
6 tablespoons (¾ stick) unsalted butter, melted
1½ cups vanilla wafer crumbs
½ cup finely chopped toasted almonds (see Note)

Filling
1 pound (2 eight-ounce packages) cream cheese, softened
8 ounces almond paste, crumbled
1 cup sugar
3 large eggs, at room temperature
1½ teaspoons vanilla extract
3 cups sour cream, at room temperature

Topping
6 tablespoons raspberry preserves
1 teaspoon lemon juice

Garnish (optional)
1 cup fresh raspberries

MAKES ONE 10-INCH CHEESECAKE

Preheat oven to 325 degrees.

To make the crust: In a small bowl, combine the butter with the vanilla wafer crumbs and the almonds. Press into the bottom of a buttered 10-inch springform pan. Bake for 10 minutes. Remove from oven and cool on rack.

To make the filling: In a large bowl, on the low speed of an electric mixer, beat the cream cheese and the almond paste until very smooth. Gradually add the sugar. Add the eggs one at a time. To ensure that the batter has no lumps and that no ingredients are stuck to the bottom of the bowl, stop the mixer several times and scrape down the sides of the bowl with a rubber spatula. Stir in the vanilla extract and the sour cream until well combined.

To make the topping: Process the raspberry preserves with the lemon juice until smooth.

Pour the batter into the prepared pan and set the pan on a baking sheet. Drop the raspberry mixture by the teaspoonful onto the top of the batter. Using the tip of a sharp knife, swirl the raspberry mixture into batter, forming a decorative pattern.

Bake until edges are set and center moves only slightly when pan is shaken, about 80 minutes. At the end of the baking time, turn off the heat, and using a wooden spoon to keep oven door slightly ajar, cool the cake in oven for 1 hour before removing. Cover and refrigerate for at least 12 hours.

Remove cake from the refrigerator at least 15–30 minutes before cutting and serving.

Garnish with fresh raspberries before cutting and serving, if desired.

NOTE: To toast hazelnuts, place on a baking sheet in a 325-degree oven for approximately 10–15 minutes or until lightly browned and fragrant.

Pies and a Cobbler

After much experimenting with crusts, crumbs, and apples, Allysa came up with this recipe as a teenager and has been making it for her family ever since.

Crust
1⅓ cups all-purpose flour
½ cup solid vegetable shortening
3 tablespoons ice water

Filling
3 tablespoons sugar
1 tablespoon all-purpose flour
⅛ teaspoon cinnamon
3 cups peeled, cored, and sliced tart apples, such as Granny Smith

Crumb Topping
2¼ cups all-purpose flour
1½ cups light brown sugar, unpacked
1 cup (2 sticks) unsalted butter, softened, cut into small pieces

Makes one 9-inch pie

Preheat oven to 425 degrees.

To make the crust: Place the flour in a large bowl and, using a pastry blender, cut in the shortening until pieces are pea-size. Sprinkle the ice water by tablespoons over the flour mixture, tossing with a fork until all the dough is moistened. Form dough into a ball. On a lightly floured surface, roll out the dough to fit into a 9-inch glass pie dish. Fold the edges under all around the rim and crimp.

To prepare the filling: In a large bowl, combine the sugar, the flour, and the cinnamon. Add the apple slices and toss gently until coated. Transfer the apple mixture into the pie crust.

To prepare the topping: In a medium-size bowl, mix together the flour and the brown sugar. Using a pastry blender, cut in the butter until the mixture resembles coarse crumbs.

Sprinkle the crumb topping over the apple mixture until well covered. Bake at 425 degrees for 10 minutes, then turn down the oven to 375 degrees and continue baking for an additional 25–35 minutes or until golden brown on top. Serve warm with sweetened whipped cream, if desired.

Blueberry Crumb Pie

There's nothing better for dessert at a summer gathering than blueberry pie. We're always asked to bring one whenever invited to a barbecue or picnic. Try this recipe with your favorite berry, or better yet, do a mix!

Crust
1⅓ cups all-purpose flour
½ cup solid vegetable shortening
3 tablespoons ice water

Filling
½ cup sugar
1½ tablespoons cornstarch
2 pints fresh blueberries

Crumb Topping
2¼ cups all-purpose flour
1½ cups unpacked light brown sugar
1 cup (2 sticks) unsalted butter, softened, cut into small pieces

MAKES ONE 9-INCH PIE

Preheat oven to 425 degrees.

To make the crust: Place the flour in a large bowl and, using a pastry blender, cut in the shortening until pieces are pea-size. Sprinkle the ice water by tablespoons over the flour mixture, tossing with a fork until all the dough is moistened. Form dough into a ball. On a lightly floured surface, roll out the dough to fit into a 9-inch glass pie dish. Fold the edges under all around the rim and crimp.

To prepare the filling: In a large bowl, combine the sugar and the cornstarch. Add the berries and toss gently until coated. Transfer the berry mixture into the pie crust.

To prepare the topping: In a medium-size bowl, mix the flour and the brown sugar. Using a pastry blender, cut in the butter until the mixture resembles coarse crumbs.

Sprinkle the crumb topping over the berry mixture until well covered. Bake at 425 degrees for 10 minutes, then turn down the oven to 375 degrees and continue baking for an additional 25–35 minutes or until golden brown on top. Serve warm with a scoop of your favorite vanilla ice cream, if desired.

Lime Pie with Gingersnap Crust

This pie is as refreshing as it is unbelievably simple. We like to use "plain ol' limes" for ours, as Key limes are not easily available throughout the year. Fellow baker Ailie Alexander came up with the cookie crust that we think makes the perfect companion to our zingy filling.

Crust
4 tablespoons (½ stick) unsalted butter, melted
1½ cups gingersnap cookie crumbs

Filling
1½ fourteen-ounce cans sweetened condensed milk
6 egg yolks
1 cup fresh lime juice (more if desired)
1 tablespoon grated lime zest

MAKES ONE 9-INCH PIE

Preheat oven to 325 degrees.

To make the crust: In a small bowl, combine the butter and the cookie crumbs. Press firmly into a 9-inch glass pie dish. Bake for 10 minutes. Remove from oven and cool on rack for 10 minutes.

To make the filling: In a medium-size bowl, on the low speed of an electric mixer, beat the milk, the yolks, and the lime juice. Taste to see if the mixture is tart enough. Add more lime juice if desired. Add the zest and incorporate. Carefully pour filling into the prepared crust. Bake for 25–30 minutes, or until the middle has set nicely.

Allow to cool for 20 minutes. Refrigerate for at least 2 hours before cutting and serving.

Pecan Pie

We tried many pecan pie recipes when we first opened the bakery. Fellow baker Kathryn McCann brought us a recipe from her Texan grandma; this recipe was the hands-down winner, and we've been serving it ever since.

Crust

1⅓ cups all-purpose flour
½ cup solid vegetable shortening
3 tablespoons ice water

Filling

⅓ cup (5⅓ tablespoons) unsalted butter, very soft
¾ cup firmly packed light brown sugar
3 large eggs, at room temperature
1 cup light corn syrup
1 teaspoon vanilla extract
⅛ teaspoon salt
1½ cups coarsely chopped pecans

MAKES ONE 9-INCH PIE

Preheat oven to 375 degrees.

To make the crust: Place the flour in a large bowl and, using a pastry blender, cut in the shortening until pieces are pea-size. Sprinkle the ice water by tablespoons over the flour mixture, tossing with a fork until all the dough is moistened. Form dough into a ball. On a lightly floured surface, roll out the dough to fit into a 9-inch glass pie dish. Fold the edges under all around the rim and crimp.

To prepare the filling: In a medium-size bowl, cream the butter and the sugar. Add the remaining ingredients, except for the pecans, in order, one at a time, beating well with each addition. Stir in half the pecans. Carefully pour filling into the prepared crust. Sprinkle the remaining pecans evenly over the filling. Bake for approximately 50–60 minutes or until filling is fairly set. (Filling will firm up as it cools.)

Allow pie to cool for 2 hours before cutting and serving. Serve with sweetened whipped cream if desired.

Here's a southern favorite that our customers clamor for, particularly around Thanksgiving. Jennifer added a few twists of her own to this durable standard to make it a delectable treat any time.

Crust

1½ cups all-purpose flour
1 tablespoon sugar
¼ teaspoon salt
8 tablespoons (1 stick) cold unsalted butter, cut into small pieces
2–3 tablespoons ice water

Filling

4 tablespoons (½ stick) unsalted butter, softened
¼ cup sugar
¼ cup firmly packed light brown sugar
1½ cups mashed sweet potato, fresh or canned, well drained
2 large eggs, at room temperature
½ cup milk
2 tablespoons bourbon
1 tablespoon vanilla extract
¾ teaspoon cinnamon
¼ teaspoon nutmeg
¼ teaspoon ginger
1 teaspoon salt

Makes one 9-inch pie

Preheat oven to 400 degrees.

To make the crust: In a large bowl, place the flour, the sugar, and the salt and, using a pastry blender, cut in the butter until pieces are pea-size. Sprinkle the ice water by tablespoons over the flour mixture, tossing with a fork until all the dough is moistened. Form dough into a ball. On a lightly floured surface, roll out the dough to fit into a 9-inch glass pie dish. Fold the edges under all around the rim and crimp.

Cover the shell with foil and line the foil with pie weights. Bake for 10 minutes. Remove from oven and carefully take out the weights and the foil. Cool on wire rack. Turn oven down to 350 degrees.

To prepare the filling: In a medium-size bowl, on the low speed of an electric mixer, cream the butter and the sugars until fluffy, about 3 minutes. Add the sweet potato, the eggs, the milk, and the bourbon and beat until well combined. Add the vanilla extract and the spices and mix well. Pour the filling into the prepared crust and bake for 45–55 minutes, until filling is fairly set or until a cake tester inserted into center of pie comes out clean.

Allow pie to cool for 30 minutes before serving.

When Allysa was growing up, her parents would host card games at their home, and friend Sally Terry would always bring one of her fabulous cheese pies. She finally divulged her secret recipe, and it became a tradition for Allysa and her mom, Geri, to bake these light custardlike pies every Christmas Eve, to be eaten the next day after Christmas dinner. The recipe calls for two pies, because as you will see, one is never enough!

Crust

12 tablespoons (1½ sticks) unsalted butter, softened
3 tablespoons sugar
3 large eggs, at room temperature
3 cups all-purpose flour
3 tablespoons baking powder

Filling

1 pound (2 eight-ounce packages) cream cheese, softened
1 cup sugar
2 tablespoons flour
2½ cups milk
1 tablespoon vanilla extract
4 large eggs, separated, at room temperature (see Note)
Juice of ½ lemon
Cinnamon sugar for sprinkling

Makes two 9-inch pies

Preheat oven to 325 degrees.

To make the crust: In a large bowl, on the low speed of an electric mixer, cream the butter and the sugar until smooth. Add the eggs and mix well. Add the flour and the baking powder, beating until just combined. Gather the dough into a ball, separate into two pieces, and wrap one piece in waxed paper and set aside. Roll out the dough on a lightly floured surface to fit into a 9-inch glass pie dish and fold the edges under all around the rim and crimp. Repeat with second half of dough in a second pie dish. Place the pie crusts on a jelly roll or cookie sheet.

To prepare the filling: In a large bowl, on the low speed of an electric mixer, beat the cream cheese, the sugar, and the flour until smooth and creamy. Add the milk, the vanilla extract, and the egg yolks, continuing to beat at low speed until well combined. Stir in the lemon juice. In a separate bowl, on the high speed of an electric mixer, beat the egg whites until soft peaks form. Gently fold the egg whites into the filling. Using a a ladle, divide the filling between the prepared pie crusts. Lightly sprinkle with cinnamon sugar.

Bake for 45 minutes, until pies are golden on top and filling is relatively set. Remove from oven and cool for 1 hour at room temperature. Refrigerate overnight before cutting and serving.

Note: It is best to separate the eggs when cold and then allow them to come to room temperature before proceeding with the recipe.

Chocolate Pudding Pie

Here's a made-from-scratch pie that's equally good with a graham cracker crust or a butter-based pastry crust, such as the crust from our Sweet Potato Pie (p. 111).

Crust

½ cup (1 stick) unsalted butter, melted
2 cups graham cracker crumbs
2 tablespoons sugar

Filling

1⅓ cups sugar
½ cup unsweetened cocoa powder
⅓ cup cornstarch
⅛ teaspoon salt
4 cups milk
1 ounce semisweet chocolate, finely chopped
1 tablespoon plus 1 teaspoon vanilla extract

MAKES ONE 9-INCH PIE

To make the crust: In a small bowl, combine the butter with the graham cracker crumbs and the sugar. Press firmly into a lightly buttered 9-inch glass pie dish. Place on a baking sheet and bake for 10 minutes.

Remove from oven and allow to cool on rack.

Meanwhile, prepare the pudding: In a medium-size saucepan, mix the sugar, the cocoa powder, the cornstarch, and the salt. Add half the milk and whisk until the mixture is smooth. Add the remaining milk and continue whisking, over medium heat, until pudding thickens and comes to a boil, about 10 minutes.

Remove from heat and add the chocolate and the vanilla extract, stirring until chocolate melts completely. Pour immediately into prepared crust. Cool for 20 minutes on wire rack and then refrigerate uncovered for at least 2 hours until chilled. Served with sweetened whipped cream if desired.

Nectarine Cobbler

A lovely, not-too-sweet summer dessert that's equally delicious with peaches. Be sure to use only the ripest in-season fruit, and serve it warm, with a scoop of vanilla ice cream or a dollop of sweetened whipped cream.

Filling
4 cups sliced nectarines
½ cup cold water
⅓ cup unpacked light brown sugar
1 tablespoon cornstarch
1 tablespoon unsalted butter

Topping
1 cup all-purpose flour
½ cup sugar
1½ teaspoons baking powder
½ cup milk
4 tablespoons (½ stick) unsalted butter, softened

Garnish
Cinnamon sugar for sprinkling

Makes one 13 x 9-inch cobbler

Preheat oven to 350 degrees.

To prepare the topping: In a medium-size bowl, stir together the flour, the sugar, and the baking powder. Add the milk and the butter and beat until smooth.

To prepare the filling: In a large saucepan, combine all the ingredients. Cook and stir over medium heat until mixture is thickened and bubbly, about 5–10 minutes. Pour into an ungreased 13 x 9-inch glass baking dish. Spoon the topping over the filling and spread carefully and evenly with a rubber spatula. Sprinkle with cinnamon sugar. Bake 30–40 minutes or until topping is lightly golden and a cake tester inserted into the center of topping comes out clean.

Icebox
Desserts

Lemon Icebox Pie

Here's a light, summery dessert for lemon lovers that's incredibly quick and easy to prepare. Just make sure you've made the Lemon Curd Filling the day before and you're all set.

Crust
½ cup (1 stick) unsalted butter, very soft
2 cups vanilla wafer crumbs

Filling
1½ cups heavy cream
1½ cups Lemon Curd Filling (recipe on page 91)

Garnish (optional)
⅓ cup fresh blueberries
Lemon slices

MAKES ONE 9-INCH PIE

To make the crust: In a small bowl, combine the butter and the vanilla wafer crumbs. Press firmly into a lightly buttered 9-inch glass pie dish. Wrap tightly with plastic and place in the freezer for 30 minutes.

Meanwhile, make the filling: In a large bowl, on the medium speed of an electric mixer, beat the heavy cream until stiff peaks form. Gently fold in the Lemon Curd. Pour into the prepared crust and chill for at least 4 hours or overnight. Garnish with berries around the edge of the pie and lemon slices if desired.

Peanut Butter Icebox Pie

Allysa combined three of her favorite ingredients—peanut butter, caramel, and Peanut Butter Cups—and with the help of fellow baker and peanut butter fan Ailie Alexander came up with this treat that's a slice of heaven!

Crust
½ cup (1 stick) unsalted butter, very soft
2 cups vanilla wafer crumbs

Filling
12 ounces (1½ eight-ounce packages) cream cheese, softened
3 tablespoons sugar
½ teaspoon vanilla extract
¾ cup heavy cream, whipped
6 Peanut Butter Cups, coarsely chopped (about 1 cup)
¾ cup smooth peanut butter
½ cup cold Caramel (recipe on page 92)

Garnish
3 Peanut Butter Cups, coarsely chopped (about ½ cup)
¼ cup finely chopped unsalted peanuts

Makes one 9-inch pie

To make the crust: In a small bowl, combine the butter and the vanilla wafer crumbs. Press firmly into a lightly buttered 9-inch glass pie dish. Wrap tightly with plastic and place in the freezer for 30 minutes.

Meanwhile, make the filling: In a large bowl, beat the cream cheese until smooth, about 2 minutes. Add the sugar gradually, continuing to beat. Add the vanilla extract. Fold in the whipped heavy cream. Then fold in the Peanut Butter Cups.

Lightly beat the peanut butter and spoon into a pastry bag fitted with a large round tip. Set aside.

Remove crust from freezer and carefully spread the Caramel in a thin layer over the bottom of the crust. Spoon half the filling on top of the Caramel. Drizzle half the peanut butter over the filling, and using a small knife, swirl into the cream cheese to create a marbleized effect (if you don't have a pastry bag, drop the peanut butter by teaspoonfuls). Repeat with second half of the filling and second half of the peanut butter. Garnish with Peanut Butter Cups and peanuts in a decorative manner.

Wrap carefully with plastic and chill overnight in the refrigerator.

Chocolate Wafer Icebox Cake

This dessert is a variation of the traditional Nabisco chocolate wafer refrigerator log. At Allysa's house it was always made round and then sliced like a regular layer cake—probably because it was much easier for children to assemble this way.

4 cups heavy cream
3 tablespoons sugar
1 tablespoon plus 1 teaspoon vanilla extract
1½ packages (13½ ounces) Nabisco chocolate wafer cookies

Makes one 8-inch cake

In a large bowl, whip the heavy cream with the sugar and the vanilla extract until soft peaks form, being careful not to overwhip. To assemble the cake: On a flat plate at least 9 inches in diameter, arrange seven wafers, with one wafer in the center and the remaining six surrounding it. Scoop about ¾ cup of the whipped cream onto the wafers and gently spread the cream in a thin layer to completely cover the cookies.

Continue to layer the wafers and the cream, making sure to end with a whipped cream layer on top. Refrigerate for at least 5 hours, or overnight, before cutting and serving.

Chocolate Pudding Trifle

Here's an easy dessert that was the result of an "accident" at the bakery one day. Some small chocolate cakes refused to come out of their pans (someone forgot to grease and flour!). Sad at the thought of throwing out all that delicious cake, Jennifer assembled layers of broken cake, pudding, whipped cream, and chocolate cookie crumbs. The results were fabulous, and many customers come back asking if any more "mistakes" have been made so they can have their terrific trifle!

Chocolate Cake

Use your favorite chocolate cake recipe or even a box of your favorite chocolate cake mix. Allow cake to cool for 15 minutes before proceeding. Break up the cake into small pieces in a large bowl.

Chocolate Pudding Filling

2 packages instant chocolate pudding mix
3 cups whole milk

Whipped Cream

2 cups heavy cream
1½ tablespoons sugar
2 teaspoons vanilla extract

Garnish

About 1 cup chocolate wafer crumbs, or chocolate-sandwich cookies, crushed into crumbs

FILLS A 6-QUART BOWL ABOUT ¾ OF THE WAY

Prepare the chocolate cake as recommended above.

To prepare the chocolate pudding filling: In a large bowl, on the medium speed of an electric mixer, beat the instant pudding and the milk for 3 minutes. Place uncovered in the refrigerator and chill until set, about 15 minutes.

Meanwhile, in a medium-size bowl, whip the heavy cream with the sugar and the vanilla extract until soft peaks form, being careful not to overwhip.

To assemble the trifle: Place ⅓ of the cake in the bottom of a large glass bowl. Place over this ⅓ of the pudding mixture, spreading evenly with a rubber spatula. Spread ⅓ of the whipped cream over this. Sprinkle with ⅓ of the cookie crumbs. Proceed in this fashion until three layers have been assembled, ending with a dusting of the cookie crumbs. Refrigerate at least 2 hours, or overnight, before cutting and serving.

Cream Cheese Chocolate Pudding Squares

This is another Christmastime favorite of ours. In the midst of all of the other cooking and baking, these are simple to prepare and loved by everyone.

Crust
1 cup flour
½ cup chopped pecans
⅓ cup (5⅓ tablespoons) unsalted butter, melted

Chocolate Pudding Filling
2 packages instant chocolate pudding mix
3 cups whole milk

Cream Cheese Filling
8 ounces (1 package) cream cheese, softened
1 cup sifted *confectioners' sugar*
1 cup heavy cream

Garnish
Whipped cream
Pecan halves (if desired)

Makes twelve 3-inch squares

Preheat oven to 375 degrees.

To prepare the crust: In a small bowl, mix the flour with the pecans and the butter. Press firmly into bottom of an ungreased 13 x 9 inch baking pan. Bake for 15 minutes. Remove from oven and cool on wire rack.

Meanwhile, prepare the fillings. To prepare the chocolate pudding filling: In a large bowl, on the medium speed of an electric mixer, beat the instant pudding with the milk for 3 minutes. Place uncovered in the refrigerator and chill until set, about 15 minutes. To prepare the cream cheese filling: In a large bowl, on the low speed of an electric mixer, beat the cream cheese until smooth, about 3 minutes. Add the sugar and beat well. In a separate bowl, beat the heavy cream until stiff peaks form. Gently fold the whipped cream into the cream cheese mixture.

When crust is cooled, spread the cream cheese filling evenly over the crust, using a rubber spatula. Then spread the chocolate pudding layer on top.

Wrap and chill for at least 2 hours or overnight. Cut into squares and serve with a dollop of whipped cream. Garnish with pecan halves if desired.

INDEX

Alexander, Ailie, 109
almond(s):
  Chocolate Cheesecake, 98–99
  Chocolate Crust, 98
  Crescent Cookies, 40
  Crunch Heath Bar Cheesecake, 97
  Crust, 97
  Oatmeal Raisin Cookies, 39
  Raspberry Marzipan Cheesecake, 103
  toasting, 39
  Vanilla Crust, 103
Amaretto Chocolate Bundt Cake, 74
apple:
  Crumb Buns, 24
  Crumb Pie, 107
  Pecan Cake, 78
  Pecan Quick Bread, 27
  Walnut Cake with Caramel-Cream Cheese Icing, 66
Apricot Coffee Cake, 76
Aunt Daisy's Fresh Fruit Torte, 79

banana:
  Chocolate Chip Peanut Loaf, 30
  Hummingbird Cake, 64
bars:
  Lemon, 45
  Magic Cookie, 56
  Strawberry Oat, 46
  see also squares
Birthday Cake, Traditional Vanilla, 60
Blondies, Peanut Butter Heath Bar, 53
blueberry:
  Crumb Pie, 108
  Muffins, 23
breads, quick:
  Apple Pecan, 27
  Blueberry Muffins, 23
  Chocolate Chip Peanut Banana Loaf, 30
  Corn Muffins, 21
  Cranberry Orange, 28
  Oatmeal Muffins, 22
  Poppy Seed, 29
breakfast treats:
  Blueberry Muffins, 23
  Chocolate Chip Peanut Banana Loaf, 30
  Corn Muffins, 21
  Dried-Cherry Crumb Buns, 24
  Glazed Breakfast Buns, 25
  Lemon Curd Filling (as spread for toast or scones), 91
  Oatmeal Muffins, 22
  Poppy Seed Bread, 29
  Poppy Seed Coffee Cake, 76
  Sour Cream Breakfast Buns, 26
  Strawberry Oat Bars, 46
brownies:
  Butterscotch Cream Cheese Swirl, 51
  Caramel Pecan, 52
  Chocolate, with Cream Cheese Icing, 49
  Fudge, with White Chocolate, Toffee, and Pecans, 50
  Peanut Butter Fudge, 54–55
  Vanilla Pecan, 48
bundt cakes:
  Chocolate Amaretto, 74
  Lemon Vanilla, 73
buns:
  Dried-Cherry Crumb, 24
  Glazed Breakfast, 25
  Sour Cream Breakfast, 26
butter, 17
  bringing to room temperature, 13
  creaming, 14
buttercream:
  Chocolate, 84
  Lemon, 85
  Mocha, 84
  Vanilla, Traditional, 83
Buttermilk Chocolate Layer Cake, 67
butterscotch:
  Cream Cheese Swirl Brownies, 51
  Filling, 90

cake pans, 13
cakes, 57–79
  chocolate, in Chocolate Pudding Trifle, 120
  Chocolate Amaretto Bundt, 74
  Chocolate Sour Cream, with Chocolate Chips, 75
  Chocolate Wafer Icebox, 119
  Dump, 77
  Fresh Fruit Torte, Aunt Daisy's, 79
  icing, 14
  Lemon Vanilla Bundt, 73
  Pear Pecan, 78
  Poppy Seed Coffee, 76
cakes, layer, 57–69
  Apple Walnut, with Caramel-Cream Cheese Icing, 66
  Chocolate Buttermilk, 67
  Coconut, 62–63
  Devil's Food, 68
  frosting, 14
  German Chocolate, 69
  helpful hints for, 13–14
  Hummingbird, 64
  Lemon, 61
  Maple Walnut, with Fluffy Maple Frosting, 65
  Vanilla Birthday, Traditional, 60
  White, Old-Fashioned, 59

Caramel, 92
Cream Cheese Icing, 66
Pecan Brownies, 52
Pecan Cheesecake, 96
Pecan Filling and Frosting, 69
cheesecakes, 93–103
Caramel Pecan, 96
Chocolate Almond, 98–99
Chocolate Swirl, 100
Crumb-Topped, 95
Heath Bar Almond Crunch, 97
helpful hints for, 16
Mocha Rum, 102
Raspberry Marzipan, 103
White Chocolate Hazelnut, 101
Cheese Pie, 112
cherry:
Dried-, Crumb Buns, 24
Dump Cake, 77
chocolate:
Almond Cheesecake, 98–99
Almond Crust, 98
Amaretto Bundt Cake, 74
Brownies with Cream Cheese Icing, 49
Buttercream, 84
Buttermilk Layer Cake, 67
Caramel Pecan Brownies, 52
-Covered Log Cookies, 34
Crust, 100, 102
Devil's Food Cake, 68
Drop Cookies with Heath Bars, Vanilla Chips, and Pecans, 35
Fudge Brownies with White Chocolate, Toffee, and Pecans, 50
German, Cake, 69
Glaze, 88
Lemon Vanilla Marble Bundt Cake, 73
melting, 34
Mocha Buttercream, 84
Mocha Rum Cheesecake, 102
Peanut Butter Fudge Brownies, 54–55
Pudding Cream Cheese Squares, 121
Pudding Pie, 113
Pudding Trifle, 120
Sour Cream Cake with Chocolate Chips, 75
Swirl Cheesecake, 100
Wafer Icebox Cake, 119
White, Coconut Macadamia Cookies, 42
White, Fudge Brownies with Toffee, Pecans and, 50
White, Hazelnut Cheesecake, 101
chocolate chip(s):
Chocolate Sour Cream Cake with, 75
Cookies, 33
Crumb Buns, 24
Magic Cookie Bars, 56
Peanut Banana Loaf, 30
Cobbler, Nectarine, 114
coconut:
Filling, 62
Layer Cake, 62–63
Magic Cookie Bars, 56
White Chocolate Macadamia Cookies, 42
Coffee Cake, Poppy Seed, 76
cookie(s), 31–42
Almond Crescent, 40
Chocolate Chip, 33
Chocolate-Covered Log, 34
Chocolate Drop, with Heath Bars, Vanilla Chips, and Pecans, 35
creating uniform crumbs out of, for crusts, 16
helpful hints for, 15
Magic, Bars, 56
Molasses, Iced, 36
Oatmeal Raisin Almond, 39
Orange Vanilla Chip, 41
Peanut Butter, 37
Peanut Butter Cup, 38
White Chocolate Coconut Macadamia, 42
Corn Muffins, 21
cranberry(ies):
Apple Pecan Quick Bread, 27
Fresh Fruit Torte, Aunt Daisy's, 79
Orange Bread, 28
Crawford, Winifred, 78
cream cheese, 17
Butterscotch Swirl Brownies, 51
Caramel Icing, 66
Chocolate Pudding Squares, 121
Icing, 87
Icing, Chocolate Brownies with, 49
creaming butter, 14
Creamy Custard Filling, Basic, 89
Crescent Cookies, Almond, 40
crumb:
Buns, Dried-Cherry, 24
Pie, Apple, 107
Pie, Blueberry, 108
Squares, Raspberry, 47
-Topped Cheesecake, 95
crusts:
Almond, 97
Chocolate, 100, 102
Chocolate Almond, 98
creating uniform crumbs out of cookies for, 16
Gingersnap, 109
Graham Cracker, 52, 113
Graham Cracker Hazelnut, 101
helpful hints for, 15–16
Pastry, Butter-Based, 15, 111, 112
Pastry, Vegetable Shortening–Based, 15, 107
Vanilla, 117, 118
Vanilla Almond, 103
Vanilla Pecan, 96
Curd, Lemon, Filling, 91
custard fillings:
Butterscotch, 90
Creamy, Basic, 89

Davis, Debra, 78
Devil's Food Cake, 68
Dried-Cherry Crumb Buns, 24
Dump Cake, 77

eggs, 17
adding to cake batter, 14
bringing to room temperature, 13
espresso:
Mocha Buttercream, 84
Mocha Rum Cheesecake, 102
extracts, 17

fillings:
Butterscotch, 90
Caramel Pecan, 69
Coconut, 62
Creamy Custard, Basic, 89
helpful hints for, 14
Lemon Curd, 91
flour, 17
sifting, 13–14
flouring cake pans, 13
Fresh Fruit Torte, Aunt Daisy's, 79
frostings:
Caramel Pecan, 69
helpful hints for, 14
Maple, Fluffy, 65
White, 62–63
see also icings
Fruit Torte, Aunt Daisy's, 79
fudge:
Brownies with White Chocolate, Toffee, and Pecans, 50
Peanut Butter Brownies, 54–55

Ganache, Chocolate, 88
German Chocolate Cake, 69
Gingersnap Crust, Lime Pie with, 109
Glazed Breakfast Buns, 25
glazes:
Chocolate, 88
Streusel, 25
Sugar, 78

graham cracker(s):
Crust, 52, 113
Hazelnut Crust, 101
Magic Cookie Bars, 56
greasing cake pans, 13

hazelnut(s):
Graham Cracker Crust, 101
toasting, 101
White Chocolate Cheesecake, 101
Heath Bar(s):
Almond Crunch Cheesecake, 97
Chocolate Drop Cookies with Vanilla Chips, Pecans and, 35
Peanut Butter Blondies, 53
Hello Dollys, 56
Hummingbird Cake, 64

icebox desserts, 115–21
Chocolate Pudding Trifle, 120
Chocolate Wafer Icebox Cake, 119
Cream Cheese Chocolate Pudding Squares, 121
Lemon Icebox Pie, 117
Peanut Butter Icebox Pie, 118
Iced Molasses Cookies, 36
icings:
Caramel-Cream Cheese, 66
Chocolate Buttercream, 84
Cream Cheese, 87
Cream Cheese, Chocolate Brownies with, 49
helpful hints for, 14
Lemon Buttercream, 85
Mocha Buttercream, 84
Seven-Minute, 86
Sugar, 36
Vanilla Buttercream, Traditional, 83
see also frostings
ingredients, 17
alternately adding, 14
bringing to room temperature, 13, 16
dry, sifting, 13–14

Kaplan, Steven, 77

layer cakes, *see* cakes, layer
lemon:
Bars, 45
Buttercream, 85
Curd Filling, 91
Icebox Pie, 117
juice, 17
Layer Cake, 61
Vanilla Bundt Cake, 73
lime:
juice, 17
Pie with Gingersnap Crust, 109
Log Cookies, Chocolate-Covered, 34

Macadamia White Chocolate Coconut Cookies, 42
Magic Cookie Bars, 56
Magnolia Bakery, 9–10
maple:
Frosting, Fluffy, 65
Walnut Layer Cake with Fluffy Maple Frosting, 65
Marble Bundt Cake, 73
Marzipan Raspberry Cheesecake, 103
McCann, Kathryn, 110
milk, 17
mocha:
Buttercream, 84
Rum Cheesecake, 102
Molasses Cookies, Iced, 36
muffins:
Blueberry, 23
Corn, 21
Oatmeal, 22

Nectarine Cobbler, 114

oat(meal):
Muffins, 22
Raisin Almond Cookies, 39
Strawberry Bars, 46

orange:
Cranberry Bread, 28
Vanilla Chip Cookies, 41

pans, cake, 13
peanut butter:
Cookies, 37
Cup Cookies, 38
Fudge Brownies, 54–55
Heath Bar Blondies, 53
Icebox Pie, 118
Peanut Chocolate Chip Banana Loaf, 30
pear:
Fresh Fruit Torte, Aunt Daisy's, 79
Pecan Cake, 78
pecan(s):
Apple Quick Bread, 27
Caramel Brownies, 52
Caramel Cheesecake, 96
Caramel Filling and Frosting, 69
Chocolate-Covered Log Cookies, 34
Chocolate Drop Cookies with Heath Bars, Vanilla Chips and, 35
Cream Cheese Chocolate Pudding Squares, 121
Dump Cake, 77
Fudge Brownies with White Chocolate, Toffee and, 50
Glazed Breakfast Buns, 25
Hummingbird Cake, 64
Pear Cake, 78
Pie, 110
Sour Cream Breakfast Buns, 26
Vanilla Brownies, 48
Vanilla Crust, 96
pie crusts, *see* crusts
pies, 105–13
Apple Crumb, 107
Blueberry Crumb, 108
Cheese, 112
Chocolate Pudding, 113
helpful hints for, 15–16
Lemon Icebox, 117
Lime, with Gingersnap Crust, 109
Peanut Butter Icebox, 118
Pecan, 110
Sweet Potato, 111
pineapple:
Dump Cake, 77
Hummingbird Cake, 64
poppy seed:
Bread, 29
Coffee Cake, 76
Orange Bread, 28
Prune Coffee Cake, 76
pudding:
Chocolate, Cream Cheese Squares, 121
Chocolate, Pie, 113
Chocolate, Trifle, 120

Raisin Oatmeal Almond Cookies, 39
raspberry:
Crumb Squares, 47
Marzipan Cheesecake, 103
Rum Mocha Cheesecake, 102

Seven-Minute Icing, 86
sifting dry ingredients, 13–14
sour cream:
Breakfast Buns, 26
Chocolate Cake with Chocolate Chips, 75
squares:
Butterscotch Cream Cheese Swirl Brownies, 51
Caramel Pecan Brownies, 52
Chocolate Brownies with Cream Cheese Icing, 49
Cream Cheese Chocolate Pudding, 121
Fudge Brownies with White Chocolate, Toffee, and Pecans, 50
Peanut Butter Fudge Brownies, 54–55
Peanut Butter Heath Bar Blondies, 53
Raspberry Crumb, 47
Vanilla Pecan Brownies, 48
see also bars
Strawberry Oat Bars, 46
sugar, 17
adding to cake batter, 14
Sweet Potato Pie, 111

Terry, Sally, 112
toffee:
Chocolate Drop Cookies with Heath Bars, Vanilla Chips, and Pecans, 35
Fudge Brownies with White Chocolate, Pecans and, 50
Heath Bar Almond Crunch Cheesecake, 97
Peanut Butter Heath Bar Blondies, 53
toppings:
Crumb, 24, 95, 107, 108
Whipped Cream, 120
Torte, Fresh Fruit, Aunt Daisy's, 79
Trifle, Chocolate Pudding, 120

vanilla:
Almond Crust, 103
Birthday Cake, Traditional, 60
Buttercream, Traditional, 83
Chip Orange Cookies, 41
Chips, Chocolate Drop Cookies with Heath Bars, Pecans and, 35
Crust, 117, 118
Lemon Bundt Cake, 73
Pecan Brownies, 48
Pecan Crust, 96

walnut(s):
Apple Cake with Caramel-Cream Cheese Icing, 66
Butterscotch Cream Cheese Swirl Brownies, 51
Chocolate-Covered Log Cookies, 34

Glazed Breakfast Buns, 25
Magic Cookie Bars, 56
Maple Layer Cake with Fluffy Maple Frosting, 65
water bath, for cheesecakes, 16
Whipped Cream, 120
White Cake, Old-Fashioned, 59
white chocolate:
Coconut Macadamia Cookies, 42
Fudge Brownies with Toffee, Pecans and, 50
Hazelnut Cheesecake, 101
White Frosting, 62–63